YOUR FREE GIFT

Thank you for choosing my book. As a special thank you, I'd like to give you my Multi-Career Starter Kit as a free gift.

You'll get:

- The Multi-Career Starter Kit eBook
- A powerful exercise including a special AI prompt
- Three different career options based on your CV
- A map template to sketch your three new options

This is one of the exercises from the book, and I'm sharing it now so you can get your new career journey started without delay.

DOWNLOAD YOUR FREE MULTI-CAREER STARTER KIT:

👉 **www.learnearnown.me/freegift**

Join thousands of professionals designing careers they truly own, not careers that own them.

If you'd like to delve deeper and access additional exclusive tools and templates, you can find them in the book.

Watch out for other content, courses and programs coming soon.

Yours,
Conor

Conor Lynch

✉ conor@conorlyn.ch

🌐 www.conorlyn.ch

🌐 TheAssetsLadder.com

SCAN ME

1

Endorsements

★★★★★

"This book is an absolute game-changer for anyone looking to take control of their financial future. The concept of a 'career assets ladder' is both practical and empowering - guiding readers step-by-step on how to build sustainable side hustles. I wish I'd read it years ago."
Alex Slattery, Career Coach, Senior HR Business Partner, Mercer.

"Insightful analysis on how the world of work has changed forever and will never be the same again. Not just for early-stage GenZ but for baby boomers like myself. This is a logical, structured approach that is really helpful." **John Whelan, Trinity College Dublin**

"It inspired me as the kind of guide I would love to have seen starting out in my career - the career guide for Gen Z and Gen Alpha!"
John Kennedy, Editor, Think Business, Bank of Ireland.

"As an experienced international business advisor, I'd recommend Conor's book to support anyone creating a personal brand or a digital business."
Dr. Domingo Sanchez Zarza. Advisor. Innovator. Mentor.

"I highly recommend this book as a recent graduate entering the real world and a tough job market. It has opened my mind greatly to the possibilities I may have for my career, rather than just a traditional 9-5. I love the AI prompts that allow ChatGPT to act as my career coach." **Tolu Onamusi**

"This is one of those books that makes you rethink how careers actually work today. The book is full of practical tools and prompts to plan your next move." **Angel Sueiro**

"The Assets Ladder is the guidebook for building freedom, not just income."
Becky Thomas, PCC, President, Be Greater Consulting, Author.

"Conor's book is an amazing resource for anyone starting anew, changing course, or looking to kick themselves up the career ladder. His work with Connector speaks for itself." **Vinnie Faneran, Deputy Editor, Reach plc**

"Conor is a pioneer when it comes to all things digital and social. His knowledge and experience are inspiring. I was a client of Conor and Connector for just over six years, both in Ireland and the UK.
Justin Costello, Marketing Director, UK & Irl. at Huawei Technologies

LEARN
EARN
OWN

THE
ASSETS
LADDER

Dedicated to:
Aisling & Daniel

First Edition Book: TAL281125

28th November 2025

Publishing this draft book is to facilitate a short period for feedback and edits before finalising the first edition.

A special thanks to my amazing proofreaders, Kathleen and Danny. Sincere thanks also to everyone else who gave me valuable feedback and support as this book came to life.

Yours,

Conor P. Lynch

www.TheAssetsLadder.com
www.conorlyn.ch

Contents

Look out for these icons

Your most valuable asset is your time.
Use your time to create valuable assets.

1. INTRODUCTION

Meet Don Leahy

As I sat in Helsinki airport waiting for a flight to a family celebration in northern Finland, I sipped my coffee nervously as it dawned on me what was happening. I was just off the phone from a live interview with Ireland's top radio station. I was introduced to the listeners as Don Leahy, a fictitious character I made up to hide my true identity.

Using the pseudonym Don Leahy, I orchestrated a grassroots marketing campaign on the Bebo social network, which captured widespread media attention. My alter-ego Don was also featured on the BBC website for the same story, the very same day. Was Don taking over my life?

What started as a nostalgic campaign by my t-shirt brand 'Conman' to resurrect a beloved Irish soft drink brand, Cavan Cola, quickly became a stressful story of personal branding and professional risk. Conman was an edgy nickname that embodied my irreverent approach to fashion.

The campaign included creating t-shirts for 'Cavan Cola', boldly using Coca-Cola's iconic white fonts, on Cavan's famous royal blue county colours. It was a delicate dance of creativity and potential job jeopardy, given that my day job was in a digital marketing agency actively working on Coca-Cola marketing in Ireland.

The inevitable collision between my corporate identity and free spirit came soon after. A provocative PR stunt featuring a parody t-shirt on national television led to my departure from this corporate job. What felt like a big career setback ended up becoming a pivotal learning opportunity.

Recognising the need for a more subtle approach, I retired the gangster inspired 'Suspiciously Good' Conman brand and launched a more career aligned personal brand called 'Connector'. For the record, this was my third personal brand website, as prior to Conman and Connector, I launched a debut Conor Lynch website over two decades ago in 1999.

If you don't have a plan, you become part of somebody else's plan.

Terence McKenna

In the early days of digital marketing, long before structured courses and micro-credentials existed, personal experimentation was my primary pathway to learning. My journey began with this audacious Conman side hustle which would become a pivotal project in understanding the power of personal branding, digital marketing, and social media. It's a reminder that the most valuable skills are often learned outside traditional employment.

This journey of discovery was never about rebellion, but instead a learning laboratory. Each idea, each personal project, and each experiment was a deliberate step in understanding the tools and techniques of the time. Long before it became a mainstream concept, I lived the philosophy of continuous learning, increased earning, and an openness to owning.

As a multi-award-winning innovator in digital business for 25 years, I built a career helping others navigate the adoption of three gigantic waves of consumer technology: the Internet, social media, and now AI. My unique career journey saw me move from 'time sheet to term sheet', from clocking in as an employee, to clocking out with a business exit.

My time working on innovative digital projects and educational experiences for global brands prepared me for creating these innovative tools and templates. Distilling so much of my career insights into a coherent career planning tool took months of experimentation. However, it's worth it to share these ideas with you.

The Future of Work is here

Fast forward to today, and traditional linear career paths are becoming increasingly obsolete. An alarming 85% of individuals report being disengaged at work. Many of these are trapped in a cycle of stress, burnout, and unfulfilling employment, which seems impossible to escape. People are living longer, changing jobs more frequently, and facing stagnating incomes while simultaneously seeking meaning, flexibility, and financial security.

For generations, the dominant career model for many has been simple: work more hours and earn more money. However, the Career Ladder model is broken - it forces you to trade time for money without building real ownership. And 'safe' careers are no longer safe.

"
50% of all professionals will have multiple income sources by 2030.

OECD

Source : OECD 2016

Work is undergoing a radical transformation that challenges everything we understand about work, careers, and making money. By 2034, the traditional 9-to-5 job is predicted to become extinct, with the concept of a "job for life" already consigned to the dustbin of history for most roles. Jobs are disappearing, and many people have no backup plan.

Influential thought leaders are painting a picture of a dramatic workforce evolution. LinkedIn co-founder Reid Hoffman predicts that independent workers will constitute 50% of the workforce within a decade, while the OECD forecasts that 50% of workers will have multiple income sources by 2035.

While many people feel trapped in the usual employment models, some escape. In 2021, the world witnessed the Great Resignation, where millions of people walked away from jobs that no longer worked for them. Headlines framed it as mass quitting, but underneath was something deeper: a collective rethinking of what work should mean.

People weren't just resigning; they were redesigning. They sought flexibility, freedom, and ownership. Many launched side hustles, moved into freelancing, or retrained in entirely new industries. It wasn't an end, it was a beginning. The lesson is clear: security doesn't come from building on rented land. It comes from building assets that create options and income on your own terms. The Great Resignation was really the first wave of a bigger shift, a move from stagnation to experimentation.

Technical innovations, particularly AI, are accelerating this transformation. Sam Altman of OpenAI suggests we might soon witness the emergence of billion-dollar, single-person companies - a concept unimaginable just a few years ago.

The Age of AI represents a significant shift in personal economic potential towards career independence. With global digital platforms, remote work capabilities, and AI-powered tools, individuals can now accomplish tasks that previously required entire teams. Virtual assistants, global freelance marketplaces, and advanced digital tools are demolishing traditional barriers to entry for startups. Now, external investment is often bypassed.

Visionary entrepreneur and writer Naval Ravikant previously speculated about a future where 7 billion unique businesses might emerge. This challenges our traditional understanding of work and entrepreneurs. He clearly envisioned the global emergence of Micropreneurs and Multipreneurs, which we witness today.

Multiply your options

Your career is probably your life's biggest investment in terms of time and money. Your potential earnings with multiple income streams would shock you if you did the calculations. Lost earnings compound daily, making early moves a big advantage in lifetime earnings.

Getting started in a career is not easy, with many working for free or for very little money to get on the Career Ladder. These work placements, internships, and apprenticeships are not ideal, with low incomes the norm. However, another way to build your own early-stage career experience is with your own Learning Projects. Even if you earn no money, you earn skills and a reputation.

The Assets Ladder is a game-changing career mapping framework that helps individuals visualise how learning, earning, and ownership build upon each other to create long-term career assets.'Learn Earn Own' is a career development model that underpins The Assets Ladder framework, describing how skills, income, and assets compound over time. I want to move you from dependence to independence.

No matter your career stage, The Asset Ladder has Career Zones and Career Roles with customised actions. Act now to see your success compound. Alternatively, each day of indecision represents a compounding loss of potential skills, income, and assets. Time has emerged as the ultimate career currency, demanding a radical shift in how we invest it. And ownership is a career multiplier.

Career options speak to what people truly want: choice, flexibility, and control over their professional destiny. It encompasses various revenue streams, multiple projects, diverse skill sets, extensive networks, and alternative career paths. Career options reduce risk and give you much-needed backup plans.

Whether you're aspiring to climb the Career Ladder, launch a side hustle, or create an entirely new career plan, the need to learn, earn, and own has never been more critical.

Instead of asking "How can I find a job opportunity?", a better question is "How can I design my career so that more opportunities come to me?" Take ownership of your career so options grow, while hours don't.

Work hours can be cut, but with a diversified career portfolio, assets can grow. The more options you create, the more resilient, adaptable, and valuable you become. Learn how to work the system rather than be worked by it.

The Future of Work demands adaptability, proactivity, and a willingness to embrace change. Whether you dream of corporate success, doing your own thing, or a hybrid career model, success begins with deliberate, strategic planning. The goal of this book is to provide new tools and thinking to transform uncertainty into opportunity.

Even if you have no qualifications or assets or money, the exciting world of your very own Career Projects is only hours away at most. No matter what your background, you can achieve more if you implement the ideas in this book. Ideas become actions become assets. Repeat.

'Learn Earn Own' turns the old model upside down. It provides you with transformative tools and templates to create personalised Career Projects and Career Assets. I want to help you identify emerging opportunities that span employment, self-employment, and collaborative partnerships. Partner with A-players, and outperform B-players to seize both a competitive and collaborative advantage.

This book developed from my research into non-traditional multi-linear careers. Hopefully, it will inspire you with fresh thinking and inspirational stories from very successful people who learned and earned while creating valuable assets.

I want others to succeed much faster than I did, and this passion led me to write this book. But I don't want you to just read, I want you to use the tools in this book to create and evaluate. And the great thing is, you don't need new billion-dollar business ideas either.

Grab a pen. Don't settle for "just okay".

Let's 'Learn Earn Own'.

Make sure you are climbing the right ladder.

2. WHY NOW?

Wasting your time and money?

Now, more than ever, it is critical to plan your career journey. and make winning moves fast. People are living longer and job-hopping more frequently, while incomes stagnate, and job satisfaction is falling.

With job security and job satisfaction in decline, more people want to take control of their careers. If you are in the 15% of employees who are engaged at work according to Gallup, congratulations. The only issue is how long you can hold onto the job before you are fired.

Disengaged working lives too often become a tragedy of wasted potential and frustration, leading to stress and money problems. Times have changed, and people like you are often motivated to be the creators of your own success. The job for life is almost dead - now you have to take control of your destiny.

Changing jobs, careers, and sectors is now more achievable and often more rewarding. Learning about new subjects and acquiring relevant skills has never been easier and can help shape a bright future. Breaking free from career stagnation means changing your approach to fit in with the changing world.

The biggest problem I see is the lack of ambition from people to try out new opportunities. The difference between a career based on one role at a time, versus managing multiple career activities, is stark. The difference is further multiplied over time for those who act without delay.

The Age of AI

Artificial Intelligence is revolutionising the world of work and brings threats and opportunities, depending on your perspective. Some say people won't lose their jobs to AI, but rather they will lose their jobs to someone using AI.

Although not a 'Digital Native' due to my demographics, in terms of psychographics, I am 'forever young'. I'm open-minded with a growth mindset and continuously trying new tools to work more smartly. Therefore, I recommend testing new tools for all aspects of your work. User-friendly AI tools offer immediate advantages in terms of speed, cost savings, and a faster route to sales revenue.

> **"Within a decade, 50% of the US population will be freelancers."**

REID HOFFMAN

LinkedIn Co-Founder / Author / Investor

STARTED AT APPLE, MANAGED OPERATIONS AT PAYPAL, CO-FOUNDED LINKEDIN, NOW OWNS A PORTFOLIO OF ASSETS.

Source : Reid Hoffman 2024

Remember the old saying about being a 'Jack of all trades, and master of none'? Is it fair to say these words of wisdom are no longer true? With AI tools helping anyone who can type to acquire incredible outputs, previously the domain of expert specialists, are we now in a golden age for generalists?

How we work is changing, and I want to explore and share the stories of pioneers in exponential potential. I want to help those who want to thrive in their chosen career(s) as the world of work sees unprecedented turbulence.

I encourage all to embrace these new tools and technologies in their personal projects. In a world where anyone can do anything, what will you do?

BEN FRANCIS
GYMSHARK 🇬🇧

He started Gymshark in 2012 at age 19 while working as a pizza delivery driver and studying at Aston University. By 2020, the brand had grown into a global fitness giant valued at over £1 billion.

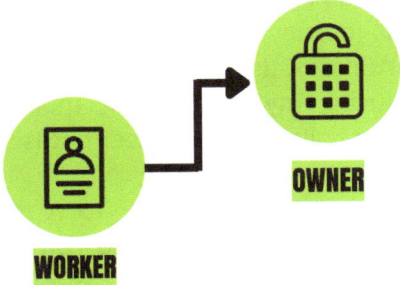

WORKER

OWNER

GYMSHARK.COM

13

Collaborative Career Design

With 85% of employees disengaged at work, the current career planning process is clearly not working and needs an upgrade. I thought it would be beneficial to incorporate some of the latest best practices in design, specifically 'Design Thinking,' into my design approach for better career outcomes. I identified that applying Design Thinking to personal planning would utilise a proven process to achieve meaningful career goals.

I label my approach 'Career Design' as it applies Design Thinking innovation principles to career development. This goes beyond traditional career planning, which is typically short-term and employment-focused.

Career Design is the personalised process of combining continuous learning and experimentation to multiply your work-life potential. With Career Design, you can create, prototype, and test multiple concurrent, collaborative career activities.

Rather than following the traditional default career path, waiting in line for jobs, you take ownership of your work to create new income streams and assets that can compound in value over time.

My approach with The Assets Ladder adds a visual framework for creating and sharing your career plans with others. When you join my workshops and webinars, you will see my Career Design ideas come to life with my experience in experience design.

While I am a big fan of The Squiggly Career idea and their careers ecosystem, I wanted to add a new approach to the visualisation of career paths. Squiggly Careers are unlike traditional linear careers, as these career journeys are more circuitous in nature, meandering to find opportunities. In my book, I want to upgrade non-linear careers by introducing my multi-linear, multi-careers approach, and also leaving room for collaborative career paths.

You must remain open to continuous iteration, adaptation, and reassessing your goals to pivot when necessary. This approach emphasises the importance of embracing lifelong learning and maintaining curiosity throughout your career journey.

Dream. Design. Deliver.

The Intelligence Economy

The knowledge economy rewarded what you knew. But today, we're entering the intelligence economy, where value comes from how quickly you can apply knowledge, adapt to change, and collaborate with AI. In this new era, human judgment, creativity, and networks combine with machine intelligence to multiply results. It's no longer enough to simply have knowledge, you need to turn that knowledge into assets you own.

That's where the Assets Ladder comes in. Instead of climbing a fragile career ladder, you build assets like skills, code, content, products, data, and ownership stakes that work for you. In the intelligence economy, those who learn to combine their unique human strengths with AI tools will own the future. The Assets Ladder gives you the playbook to diversify, multiply, and design a career that thrives in this new age of intelligence.

What differentiates people isn't access to information - it's how you use your limited time to apply knowledge to create value for yourself and others. Here are some options:

- **Time** - sell your time for money as a worker
- **Products/Services** - sell or resell products/services
- **Audience** - sell access to an audience you own
- **Assets** - earn from your assets

I will suggest more options on how to make money later, but for now, I will use online education as an example. Why? Well, because the demand for continuous learning is accelerating as people move beyond traditional career paths, developing new skills for recent opportunities like personal branding, content creation, and social media. Managing your skill stack and career should be an important part of our continuous professional development.

The creator-economy market is forecast to double from $250 to $480 billion by 2027.

Goldman Sachs

People are finding and teaching each other directly, bypassing traditional educational institutions. Instead, they're using marketplaces like Udemy, Gumroad, and Shopify to sell knowledge and solutions to one another. Many simply sell their experience solving problems to those a few steps behind them on similar paths.

The next phase of education will be personalised education delivered by AI. However, coming up with big ideas is still a way for you to use the power of AI to bring them to life. The Assets Ladder highlights this shift - it's a framework, an information product, and a practical example of the asset-building concepts discussed in this book.

A framework, model, or system can be as small as a three-step process. Do this, then this, and this to get this result. I designed a branded framework with a clear name, logo, and supporting micro-learning materials. It demonstrates how an asset ecosystem can encompass eBooks, courses, planners, events, apps, tools, and templates, etc.

KATE HORTON
MISS EXCEL

Miss Excel, also known as Kat Norton, is a former corporate consultant turned successful entrepreneur through her online Excel courses. As the founder of Miss Excel LLC, she trains millions of users via TikTok and sells her programs from Arizona.

WORKER

OWNER

MISS-EXCEL.COM

THE AGE OF AI

Greg Isenberg: If you want more out of your career, READ this:

The old path was linear: school → job → savings → retirement.
The new path is convergent: skills + assets + audience → optionality.

We keep applying industrial-age career advice to an AI-powered economy, and it's causing millions to live unhappy professional lives. I think the most valuable people today are the convergence players building three things simultaneously:

1. Skills: vibe coding, vibe marketing etc. UNDERSTAND THE TOOLS (Replit, V0, ChatGPT etc.) like a wizard. Not just content creation, but AI-human collaboration. Not just management, but community orchestration.
2. Assets: digital products, content libraries, data moats, and micro-SaaS tools that generate income while you sleep and appreciate over time.
3. Audience: direct relationships with people who trust you, bypassing platforms, institutions, and algorithms.

The magic happens at the intersection. Your audience adopts your assets. Your assets showcase your skills. Your skills attract your audience.

This is why the designer with 50,000 X followers can launch a $500K product with a single tweet while the better designer sends out desperate job applications. This is why the developer with 3 tiny SaaS products making $2K/month each has more leverage than the senior engineer earning $250K at Google. This is why the writer building an email list while ghostwriting for executives has more security than a career journalist.

The system isn't designed to teach this approach. Universities, HR departments, and even venture capital still operate on linear achievement metrics. They want to know where you went to school, where you worked, or how fast you're growing in a single dimension.

BUT THIS IS WHAT FIRES ME UP. The opportunity has never been greater for those who see it. The tools to build skills, create assets, and grow an audience are more accessible than at any point in history.

The future is bright.

" There are almost 7 billion people on th planet. Someday, I hope, there will be almost 7 billion companies.

NAVAL RAVIKANT

nav.al

Entrepreneur / Investor / Aut

STARTED IN SOFTWARE, MASTER
STARTUPS AT EPINIONS, CO-FOUN
ANGELLIST, AND NOW OWNS
A PORTFOLIO OF ASSETS.

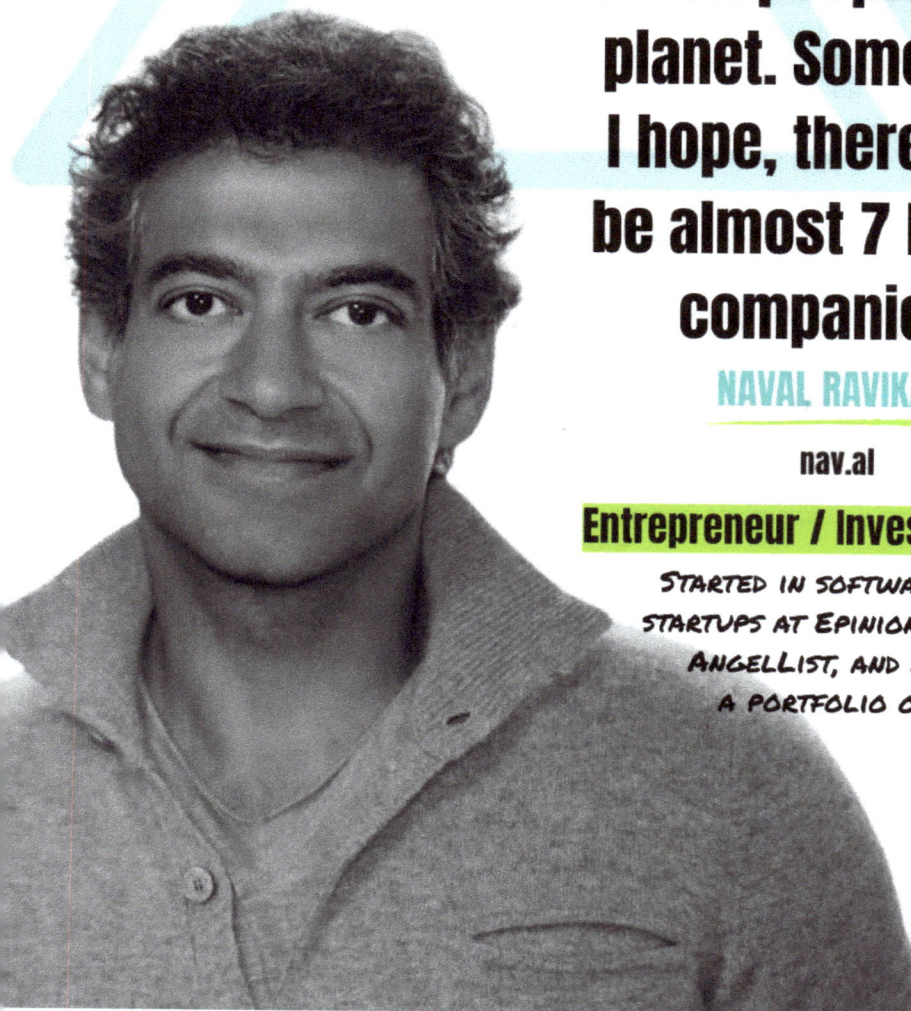

3. WHY YOU?

Why are you here?

It's not your fault. You've been told that the only path to success is working hard, waiting in line, staying loyal, and climbing the career ladder. But the world changed, and unfortunately, no one updated the Career Ladder. Until now.

Jobs don't reward long-term loyalty anymore. Schools didn't teach you how to build assets. Career advisors generally don't either but now they will have this book to help them help you. In hindsight, it would be better if we all knew there is a good chance the jobs we seek won't pay much, won't last long, and chances are we won't enjoy them.

So you weren't wrong, but as times change, you were on the wrong path with the wrong directions. Now, there's a better way. It's time to take back control with a smarter system. One that multiplies your influence, impact, and income. One that's built on owning, not serving. You don't need to climb someone else's ladder; you can create your own. Today.

Here are the most common career struggles:

Stuck in a job: lack of growth, unclear next step.
Fear of the future: AI, automation, layoffs, pensions disappearing.
Disengagement: tired of corporate life, seeking meaning.
Money stress: month-to-month living, not enough savings.
Desire for freedom: want to build something for themselves.
Confusion: not sure what to do, don't know where to start.
Side hustle itch: want to test ideas but don't know how.
Comparison trap: seeing peers succeed online, but "what about me?"

Those afraid of change with limiting beliefs and a fixed mindset tend to settle for wasting time on unfulfilling work and careers, sadly blind to their potential chances to grow. If you have no idea what you like or what you want to do, it may be advisable to try some personality tests like 'StrengthsFinder' to aid your self-discovery process.

However, if you're ready to take control of your career journey and create a strategic path forward, this book offers the blueprint you need. Whether you're looking to accelerate your current career, transition to something new, or create a portfolio of professional activities, my new approach provides the tools, guidance, and inspiration to help you succeed.

What do you do?

This is one of the first questions we ask each other, as what we do helps define how we are seen in the world. You may have found your career by accident, ending up in a dead-end job or a dying sector. However, you can change things.

Instead of accidental careers, I want to help you actively plan and manage your career like a pro in the short and long term. Ideally, you're resourceful, ambitious, and determined to make things happen rather than waiting for opportunities to find you.

This book is designed for people who want to take control of their career destiny by planning their career path more strategically. You should be seeking opportunities that fit into your career plan. This way, you'll be happy on your long-term career path by design, not by accident.

Here are some of the people who will benefit from the new ideas in this book:

- Career transitioner considering career changes
- Professional seeking acceleration
- Exploring self-employment e.g. freelancer or contractor
- Person returning to traditional employment
- Career starter or recent graduate
- Career professional seeking new tools for new careers

Some seek to climb the career ladder faster, while others desire additional income options and fulfilling passion projects. The motivation for embracing change can be as pressing as financial necessity, where current earnings are no longer sufficient to cover the high cost of living. Other motivations can include concerns about the future of work for you and your family, especially with the job losses that are expected to continue in the Age of AI.

Your journey might include several twists and turns, but ultimately, having a plan acting as a 'career compass' will help steer you in the right direction for long-term rewards.

Manage your career like a business

Helen from HR is not going to help you find a new career or start a side hustle. Rob the recruiter wants the 9-5 life for you. Your career is your business. Independent workers share a common trait: they manage their careers like a business, making a living by strategically selling their time, products, or services.

This model is particularly valuable for those who embrace self-directed learning, seek support from like-minded individuals, and want to learn from others' successes and failures. It's for people willing to navigate through uncertainty and self-doubt, and who are prepared to dig deep and discover their infinite personal potential.

With The Assets Ladder, you'll learn to identify your personal powers and develop realistic plans to achieve your career goals and make informed decisions about your future. You'll discover how to navigate various career stages effectively, create multiple income streams when desired, and build a career path that evolves with your objectives.

WILFRED EMMANUEL-JONES
THE BLACK FARMER

Wilfred Emmanuel-Jones, a former BBC producer, launched The Black Farmer while still working in media. His food brand became a success, now worth millions and sold in major UK supermarkets.

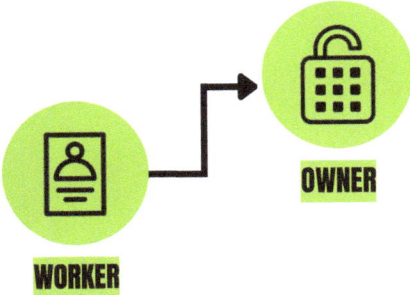

WORKER

OWNER

THEBLACKFARMER.COM

If you want to take control of your career development and make informed decisions about your future, you can benefit from a more modern and agile approach. A future that's built on owning, not serving.

In this book, I will help you with a framework for self-discovery, ideation, experimentation, and acceleration. The first step is critical. Take it and you have broken through the mental barriers holding you back. Enjoy new momentum and motivation. Resist it, and the feeling of being stuck grows, causing even more frustration and self-doubt.

It's important to acknowledge that The Assets Ladder isn't for everyone. The journey involves facing challenges like uncertainty and self-doubt, temporary confusion, frustration with the pace of progress, the need for deep self-reflection, and continuous adaptation and growth.

Become a self-starter today

A self-starter is defined as someone who begins work or undertakes projects on their own initiative, showing a proactive attitude toward tasks and challenges.

Self-starters enjoy greater flexibility, the autonomy of being their own boss, better work-life balance, chances to learn, more meaningful work, and a feeling of empowerment.

The very best investment
by far is anything
that develops yourself.

Warren Buffett

While I don't focus on mindset in this book, today's ambitious workers are increasingly independently minded and seeking career flexibility such as:

- Juggling multiple roles
- Pursuing side hustles
- Transitioning to self-employment
- Changing careers and sectors
- Seeking additional income streams
- Developing passion projects

You will learn to bypass and overcome obstacles that might have stopped you in the past. It is this resourcefulness and resilience that help people succeed. If it were easy, everyone would be doing it. I personally don't let obstacles and risks deter me. I like to pioneer new routes and have confidence I can navigate around any potential roadblocks.

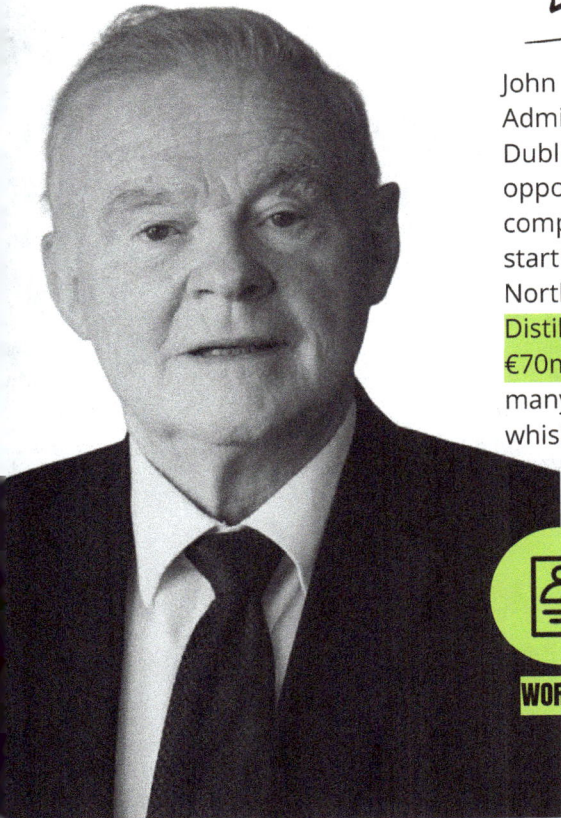

JOHN TEELING
GREAT NORTHERN DISTILLERY

John was a lecturer in Business Administration at University College Dublin while researching opportunities like exploration companies and distilleries. His startups included Cooley and Great Northern Distillery. He sold Cooley Distillery to Jim Beam for more than €70m in 2011. John is considered by many to be the 'Father of the Irish whiskey renaissance'.

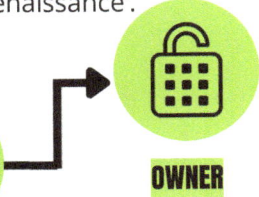

WORKER

OWNER

" **85% of global employees are** <mark>disengaged at work,</mark> **costing $8.8T in 2023.**

GALLUP

G

Source : GALLUP 2023

4. THE CAREER LADDER

The 100 year old career relic

The term Career Ladder was first used in the early 20th century, though the precise origin and the first recorded use are somewhat difficult to pinpoint. It's believed that the term began gaining popularity in the United States during the 1920s and 1930s when the concept of structured career paths within organisations started to emerge more prominently.

The idea of a Career Ladder or 'Corporate Ladder' metaphorically represents a progression of steps or stages that one would climb in their professional life, akin to the rungs of a ladder. This concept reflected the growing industrial and corporate structures of the time, where employees could advance through various roles and responsibilities within a company.

The term gained more widespread usage in the mid-20th century, especially with the rise of corporate culture, as organizations began offering more structured advancement opportunities for their employees. The idea of moving up the "career ladder" became associated with the broader notion of upward mobility, where individuals could progress professionally based on merit, skills, and experience.

While there isn't a single pinpointed source or event marking the first use of "career ladder," it was closely tied to the evolving workplace environment during the early to mid-1900s, which emphasised job security, promotions, and employee retention strategies within corporations. It can be argued that workers don't see the promised benefits of the Career Ladder being delivered in reality.

The Career Ladder model is limited by its rigid, linear structure. The model assumes a linear path upwards in a stable organisation - a reality vanishing for millions of workers. If you are determined and love the work you do, you can get to the CEO level as Indra Nooyi did in 2006, but it's not always easy.

The upward progression within a single path fails to account for the lateral moves, diverse experiences, and non-linear trajectories prevalent in modern careers.

Perhaps most critically, the Career Ladder places your professional destiny in someone else's hands. You can only climb as high as the organisation allows, at the pace they dictate, and along the exact path they've designed. In today's dynamic economy, surrendering this much control over your livelihood is increasingly risky.

The stability of the Career Ladder for many is increasingly precarious, with decreasing job security due to the advances of technology like AI and Automation. Remaining solely on the Career Ladder implies staying as a worker, primarily trading time for money. This is no longer the only approach, as this book will demonstrate.

The model still relies on organisational permanence in an era where companies rise and fall at unprecedented speeds. It suggests that value comes primarily from titles and position rather than skills, networks, and intellectual property you own.

The current world of work is too unpredictable, fast-moving and ever-changing for the Career Ladder approach to still be the most popular career planning concept.

Yet we cling to this outdated metaphor despite its growing limitations. However, as the Career Ladder is 100 years old, and the world is unrecognisable from that era, it is time to upgrade to The Assets Ladder concept.

Working hard for something we don't care about is called stress. Working hard for something we love is called passion.

Simon Sinek

Don't rely on the Career Ladder

The following are some of the reasons to look beyond the Career Ladder:

Single point of failure risk – your entire professional identity and income stream depend on one profession's stability

Limited control over advancement pace – promotions happen on the company's timeline, not yours, often requiring years of waiting, regardless of your abilities

Skills gap vulnerability – focusing only on skills valued by your current employer can leave you unprepared if you suddenly need to find work elsewhere

Deferred value capture – trading your best working years for the promise of future rewards that may never materialise if your fortunes change

Organisational ceiling – your growth is constrained by the size and structure of your organisation, regardless of your potential

Decreased employer loyalty – companies increasingly prioritise shareholder value over employee development, making long-term career promises less reliable

Technology displacement risk – specialised roles within traditional career paths are often the first targets for AI and automation replacement

Network limitation – building relationships primarily within one organisation creates a dangerously narrow professional network

Identity fragility – tying your professional identity too closely to a specific role or company creates vulnerability during transitions

Income growth constraints – salary increases typically follow standardised organisational patterns rather than reflecting your true market value

Innovation penalty – traditional ladders often reward conformity over creativity, limiting opportunities for innovative thinkers

Industry disruption blindness – being focused on one ladder can prevent you from seeing transformative changes happening nearby

Learn it. **Earn** it. **Own** it.

Take ownership of your work: climb **The Assets Ladder**.

5. MULTI-LINEAR CAREERS

It's time for new career models

As you've just seen, careers used to be so straightforward that a ladder was the perfect metaphor. Careers traditionally had linear paths flowing from education to employment. Overall, while some people are staying on the Career Ladder, many are not.

The more adventurous workers may have had non-linear careers, which have a number of different roles and sectors. Non-linear careers are becoming the norm as they offer flexibility, variety, and potentially greater rewards in a rapidly evolving work environment.

However, I believe that it is no longer simply a choice between linear or non-linear career paths, as you can have multiple simultaneous activities. So I coined this approach as 'multi-linear' or 'multilinear' careers. Today, you're not limited to a single career path, in fact the number of paths is unlimited.

This new approach encourages you to:

- Sketch multiple career options for Personal and Partner Projects
- Create, calculate, and evaluate potential outcomes
- Develop multiple income stream ideas
- Build flexible career plans

The number of people with documented multi-year career plans is vanishingly small. It's just not done. This is probably because careers were simpler, and the planning tools were not popularised.

We're at the golden age of career planning, where people will open their eyes to the other options and opportunities available to them. You do not need to be a genius or laden down with expensive qualifications to get ahead today.

An income stream can be generated from being Workers, Partners, or Owners, while many get stuck on the first option. This is changing. Fast.

The Assets Ladder represents a more flexible and contemporary model for career development. My vision is to enable users to move seamlessly between multiple different career activities, reflecting the fluid nature of modern careers.

Today, having the right tools for personal planning is more crucial than ever. This book aims to bridge the gap between traditional career planning and the modern reality for workers, providing you with practical methods to reach your goals.

Through guided exploration and strategic planning, you'll be better equipped to build a career that not only succeeds in today's turbulent times but continues to evolve and grow.

Realising one's personal potential is not just about professional advancement - it's about achieving personal fulfillment, financial stability, and creating a meaningful impact in your sector.

Whether you're starting your career, accelerating your current path, or contemplating a change, The Assets Ladder model will help you plan based on your unique situation. You can adopt a growth mindset, spotting openings for progression, and develop realistic plans to achieve your career goals.

Multi-linear career paths are where multiple career activities are simultaneous rather than subsequent.

Map your future

A career path refers to one's career journey, potentially traversing industries, jobs, or other self-employment opportunities. Whether you'd like to advance in your current career or switch to a completely different field, careful planning and execution are critical to success.

My model is designed to help you succeed faster, no matter where you are on your career journey. No two people's journeys are the same, and my career plan templates are designed to help you create a custom career plan tailored to your own needs and goals.

The Assets Ladder allows workers to plot their current position and strategise future moves across different Career Roles, providing a clear, actionable framework for designing their career.

This new approach is grounded in a fundamental belief that every worker has the power to design, redesign, and continually evolve their career. No circumstance is permanent, and every day is an opportunity for growth and strategic repositioning. I want to help you reach hero levels of greatness in your life.

The Assets Ladder model introduces an innovative visualisation tool that maps career development across two dimensions: a horizontal timeline and a vertical ownership progression. In the following pages, you can see this in more detail, and the overall Multi-Careers Model too.

THE BIG PICTURE

To get the most from this book, it is useful to understand these terms, and how they interact with each other. Here's the big picture.

Design Thinking

Design Thinking is a modern approach to innovation. It helps you understand what people really need, then create solutions that work for them and also work for your business. The DVF Framework looks for the sweet spot where the best ideas are Desirable, Feasible and Viable.

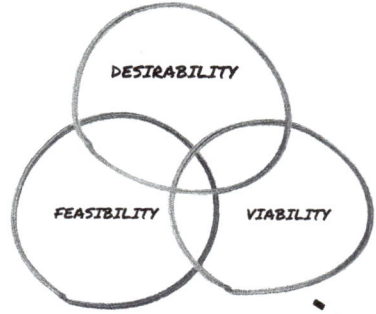

Career Design

Career Design, inspired by Design Thinking, is an innovative approach to planning your work life, achieved by understanding your needs and exploring all income possibilities. The goal is to craft a career that aligns with who you are, who you want to be, and guided by what you value.

Multi-Careers Model

The Multi-Careers Model is an innovative five-step Career Design framework to help you multiply your career potential by creating Desirable, Feasible, and Viable career activities. The model's career stages are A. Direction, B. Exploration, C. Navigation, D. Activation, and E. Evolution.

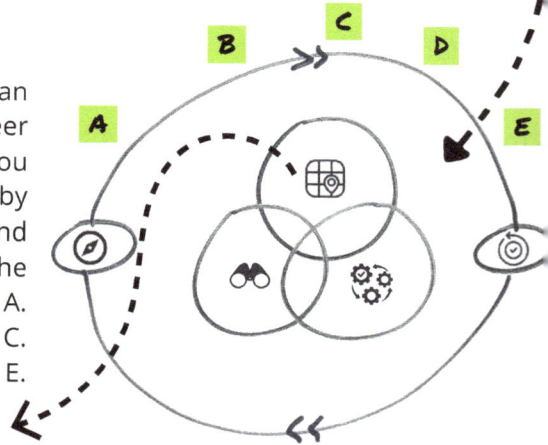

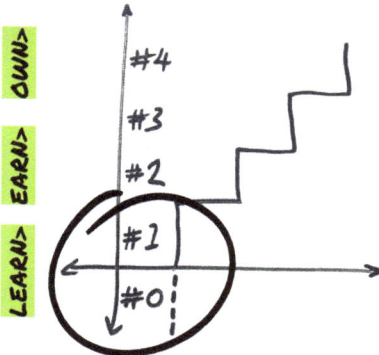

The Assets Ladder

This mapping model is from the Navigation phase, as it helps you design personalised career projects. No matter whether you work for yourself, for others, or with others, the model maximises your lifetime earnings and assets potential. Create 'Learn Earn Own' Career Projects alone or with partners.

6. MULTI-CAREERS MODEL

The Multi-Careers Model for Career Design

The Assets Ladder is part of the Multi-Careers Model. It is the third section, called Navigation, where the multi-linear careers come to life with the possibility for multiple career activities and moves.

DIRECTION
ESTABLISH YOUR GOALS
Where are you now, and where do you want to be?

EXPLORATION
RESEARCH YOUR POTENTIAL
Explore opportunities in line with your desired outcome.

NAVIGATION
MAP YOUR MOVES
Strategically plan and manage multiple career moves.

ACTIVATION
TEST & LEARN
Run small experiments to get real-world engagement.

EVOLUTION
REVIEW YOUR PROGRESS
Evolve your goals and performance during this timeline.

1. DIRECTION - Define Your North Star

Before you build anything valuable, you need a clear sense of where you're headed — and why it matters. Define Your North Star helps you uncover your deeper motivations, personal values, and vision of success, so you're no longer reacting to opportunity, but creating it. It's not about fitting into a job title — it's about designing a direction that fuels long-term meaning, freedom, and momentum.

2. EXPLORATION - Scan the Horizon

You can't discover breakthrough paths by walking the same road as everyone else. In Scan the Horizon, you'll look beyond conventional roles to explore emerging industries, interests, and income models that align with your strengths. This phase is about expanding your awareness, testing your curiosity, and uncovering overlooked opportunities that could redefine what's possible in your career.

3. NAVIGATION - Plot Your Moves

The old career ladder is gone - today, you need a map. In Plot Your Moves, you'll learn how to evaluate options, weigh risks, and design a flexible plan based on clarity, not chaos. Using a strategic approach, this phase helps you open your mind to new options, prioritise what matters, and start making career bets that build long-term leverage.

4. ACTIVATION - Make it Real

Ideas don't change lives - execution does. Make it Real is where you stop planning and start building: your first side project, your next gig, your upgraded presence, your prototype hustle. It's about testing ideas in the wild, making small bets, and getting valuable feedback that turns potential into momentum. This is where real-world assets start to take shape.

5. EVOLUTION - Evolve Your Edge

In today's fast-moving world, staying still means falling behind. Evolve Your Edge is about continuous, intentional growth — upgrading your skills, refining your systems, and stretching into new territory before the market forces you to do so. This phase is where you turn momentum into mastery. Through reflection, feedback, and focused reinvention, you'll learn how to stay relevant, increase your strategic value, and design a career that compounds in capability, confidence, and income over time.

Careers are multi-dimensional.

The origins of the Multi-Careers Model

Career options are growing in number and can range from multiple part-time jobs to full-time positions, and from freelance work to creating a startup, but the current tools don't address multiple career activities, until now.

Career planning has become infinitely more challenging in this era of juggling jobs, side hustles, and going solo. It has become obvious that most people are not naturally skilled at planning their next moves and managing their careers. For those who can afford a career coach, you may be fortunate enough to receive valuable assistance with traditional career planning and decision-making. Unfortunately, as a result, many just drift along without direction or purpose in jobs in which they are disengaged.

The origin of the model was a series of interviews conducted with some of Ireland's most recognisable personal brands. Many undertook a similar career journey from employment to simultaneous self-employment, which was very insightful.

What became strikingly apparent to me was the significant limitations of current career planning tools to address the complexities of modern career strategy and mapping. If only there were a modern tool for modern careers. Well, now there is.

While I didn't set out to replace traditional tools entirely, I recognised a significant gap in the toolbox for a tactical tool to help those seeking a practical method to create work-life plans.

The Multi-Careers Model is an innovative and collaborative Career Design model, aiming to help you multiply your career potential. This is achieved by adopting an experimental approach perfect for those who are open to opportunities in employment, self-employment, or both.

Why is maximising your career potential so important? By fully utilising your skills and talents, you can experience a greater sense of satisfaction in your work and potentially earn a higher income, achieve long-term goals, and build valuable professional relationships.

You're an asset.
Invest in yourself.

More about the Multi-Careers Model

Unlike existing models, this new model encourages individuals to explore multiple different career options and to visualise new possibilities in both the short and long term.

The Assets Ladder represents a more flexible and contemporary model for career development. My vision is to enable users to move seamlessly between multiple different career activities, reflecting the fluid nature of modern careers.

Today, having the right tools for personal planning is more crucial than ever. This book aims to bridge the gap between traditional career planning and the modern reality for workers, providing you with practical methods to reach your goals.

It is important to consider multiple career activities so you can evaluate a mix of employment, self-employment, and partnership opportunities. My new method encourages you to map multiple starting points, multiple finishing points, and multiple paths. This helps you to make informed decisions and develop a realistic plan to achieve your career goals.

I want to help you identify and compare income from relevant, profitable jobs, career openings, and potentially a profitable side hustle or business. By creating personalised career maps and action plans, your chances of career success are greatly increased.

The Multi-Careers Model, which includes The Assets Ladder in phase 3, builds upon IDEO's popular Desirability (is it wanted), Viability (is it profitable), Feasibility (can you do it) (DVF) framework. Everything you work on should have:

A - Goals - Direction
B - Desirability - Exploration
C - Viability - Navigation
D - Feasibility - Activation
E - Review - Evolution

My model has two new additions to the original DVF framework, namely setting goals at the start (A) and reviewing performance at the end (E).

The Multi-Careers Model

7. WHAT ARE ASSETS?

The role of Assets

It is time to learn more about a new model to plan your careers. First up is to learn more about 'Assets', and later I will introduce you to The Assets Ladder concept.

Two of the key variables running throughout your career are Income and Assets. Income is still fairly straightforward, but the number of ways for you to make an income has grown a lot.

Meanwhile, in the past, Assets of value were mostly owned by the rich. During my lifetime, with the digital revolution, the ownership of Assets has opened up. So I want to show you how to 'be, build, and buy' income-generating Assets which can be with the goal of both learning and earning.

Moving beyond focusing only on an employee's salary,   we move on to personal finance and wealth creation through building up your career Assets that generate income and value over time.

Types of Assets

Assets are income-generating or value-building resources that you own, create, or leverage to increase your earning potential.

In The Assets Ladder, it's important to recognise the distinction between Career Assets and financial assets - both play crucial roles in long-term wealth development.

Financial Assets: These are wealth-building tools, such as investments, property, and savings, that generate and accumulate wealth.

Career Assets: These are a combination of intangible tools (such as skills, relationships, and opportunities) and tangible resources (like products, services, tools, or intellectual property) that enhance your professional value and growth. Career Assets help you navigate your career, elevate your work, and increase your future earning potential.

Be your own boss.

Career Assets, or 'Assets' in this book, help shape your professional life by creating opportunities, enhancing your value in the job market, and positioning you for success. As you develop these assets, they set the stage for you to leverage your work into future financial success.

Types of assets that grow income

FINANCIAL ASSETS	Investments that grow in value or yield returns	Example Stocks, bonds, funds, rental property
BUSINESS ASSETS	Systems, tools, or intellectual property that earn money	Example: Online courses, software, products
PERSONAL BRAND	Your reputation, visibility, and authority	Example: Speaking gigs, book deals, sponsorships
SKILLS & KNOWLEDGE	Valuable, marketable capabilities	Example: Coding, negotiation, design, leadership
NETWORKS	Relationships that create opportunities	Example: Partnerships, referrals, collaborations
DIGITAL ASSETS	Scalable, monetisable content or platforms	Example: Content, code, community, audience etc.

You can invest your profits from Career Assets in Financial Assets.

The richest people don't trade their time for money, they trade their time for assets.

Steven Bartlett

What assets can you make?

One of the best ways to understand what assets are and how to create them for yourself is set out in Daniel Priestley's book '24 Assets'. This book is written for both aspiring and established business owners who want to build long-term value from their work and create a successful business with assets.

In his book, Priestley explains that businesses need strong overall assets across all 24 categories to stay protected in both booms and busts. The 24 assets are subdivided into both physical and softer assets, and there are 7 different asset categories:

- Intellectual property
- Brand assets
- Market assets
- Product assets
- System assets
- Culture assets
- Funding assets

Most people create a business that is overly dependent on themselves. They make sales, derive a regular income, and grow, but when they decide to take a long holiday or get sick, the business ceases to deliver the offering or generate new revenues.

This is when many realise their business doesn't have any value without them running the service and sales.
It is much better to create something where you can get others to help you with shared revenue.

Income, in its broadest definition, encompasses all monetary and non-monetary value received by an individual or entity through various channels, including traditional employment wages, salaries, bonuses, and benefits. It can also include self-employment revenue from business ownership, freelancing, consulting, or gig work.

The key to growing your 'personal stock price' is learning high-value skills that solve real problems.

Ali Abdaal

24 Assets

In his book '24 Assets', Daniel Priestley emphasises the importance of developing business assets under the following categories.

INTELLECTUAL PROPERTY: The business lays claim to, or is known for, valuable ideas, methods or defensible intellectual property rights.

- Content (books, videos, podcasts, etc.)
- Methodology (unique processes or approaches)
- Registered Intellectual Property (trademarks, patents)

BRAND ASSETS: The business is known, liked, and trusted by a loyal group of fans who are unlikely to switch to a new brand.

- Philosophy (core beliefs, mission)
- Identity (visual branding, logos)
- Ambassadors (brand advocates, influencers)

MARKET ASSETS: The business can sell products, disseminate ideas or be present to a large group of potential buyers faster and more cheaply than others in the same market.

- Positioning (unique market position)
- Channels (distribution and communication channels)
- Data (customer and market data)

PRODUCT / SERVICES ASSETS: The business has created unique products and services that are either difficult to replicate or difficult to compete with.

- Gifts (free offerings for prospects)
- Products-for-Prospects (entry-level products)
- Core Products (main revenue drivers)
- Products-for-Clients (upsells, advanced products)

SYSTEMS ASSETS: The business has a set of systems and processes that allow it to run more efficiently than its rivals while still delivering the same or better quality.

- Marketing System (automated marketing processes)
- Sales System (repeatable sales processes)
- Management System (leadership and management structure)
- Operational System (day-to-day workflows)

CULTURE ASSETS: The business is able to attract, retain, develop, and manage good people at a lower cost than its competitors.

- Key People of Influence (leaders and experts)
- Sales & Marketing Team (talent in customer acquisition)
- Management Team (leadership roles)
- Technicians (specialist staff)

FUNDING ASSETS: The business can raise capital or borrow money on better terms than its competitors.

- Business Plan (formalised strategy)
- Valuation (independent business valuation)
- Structure & Risk Mitigation (legal and financial frameworks)

Career Income

This is the money that flows into your life from both work and assets. It includes salaries, freelance fees, and side hustles, but also royalties, product sales, and even the exit or sale of an asset you've created. The stronger and more diversified your income sources, the more resilient your career becomes.

Career Investment

Career investment is the time, energy, and money you put into building your skills, networks, and opportunities. This can mean taking courses, purchasing new software, electronic devices and the tools of your trade. Like financial investments, these compound over time, paying dividends in higher earnings, stronger assets, and greater freedom.

Career Assets

These are the long-term, recurring sources of value you create: intellectual property, digital products, personal brands, equity stakes, and relationships that open doors. Unlike income, which stops when you stop working, assets continue to grow and deliver value long after the work is done. They are the foundation of true career independence.

Personal career generated assets encompass the complete portfolio of tangible and intangible resources accumulated through one's professional journey, including specialised knowledge, technical expertise, and wisdom gained through experience; professional networks, relationships, and social capital that provide access to opportunities and information.

Your assets may include Intellectual property such as methodologies, frameworks, patents, and creative works; digital assets, including online platforms, followers, and content libraries.

Other assets include Personal Brand recognition, documented accomplishments such as publications, portfolios, credentials, like degrees, certifications, and licences that validate competencies and professional reputation.

Career Assets Scorecard -> Tools & Templates chapter

Do it once,
earn multiple times.

Your career as an asset engine

In the future, according to David Autor, Professor of Economics at the Massachusetts Institute of Technology (MIT), relying solely on one's knowledge may not be sufficient for financial stability. Instead, individuals who own valuable assets will be better positioned to thrive economically.

His prediction highlights a shift in economic dependence from knowledge-based skills to asset ownership in the Age of AI. It emphasises that in the emerging economy, those who own assets will have a significant advantage over those who only possess knowledge.

"The choice is stark: Own assets or become obsolete. In Autor's future, your knowledge won't pay the bills. Your assets will. The shift is already happening. The people who own will always outperform the people who know', writes influencer Tim Carden on X.

The beauty of having assets is that you may be able to sell them on. For those in business, an 'exit strategy' is a well-recognised term for your ultimate goal with the business. Is the goal to sell it, or share it with others?

This idea for exiting your career is quite novel but makes a lot of sense as more people create more ownable assets during their careers. If you have a Personal Brand, a Personal Business, and other assets, there may be a move to pass these assets to others before you quit working altogether.

Earlier in my career, I already exited the Connector business, so I like to think I will have some assets to share or sell when I decide I've worked enough for one lifetime. These could include domain names, brands, information products, intellectual property, books, tools, databases, and knowledge bases, or similar. Think in terms of assets, and start to climb The Assets Ladder.

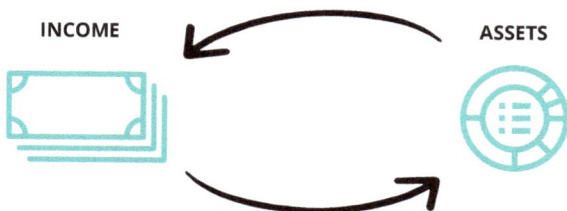

INCOME   ASSETS

8. THE ASSETS LADDER

From one job to multiple assets

What if everything you were told about careers like the Career Ladder is no longer relevant? This old model just isn't working any more. But what will you replace it with? I know—the Assets Ladder.

As we learned, there are financial assets and career assets, now let's look at The Assets Ladder. This is presented as a new metaphor for creating personal assets. It illustrates the progression from Workers with no assets, to Partners and Owners who have assets. The core idea is to build resources that generate income or value beyond directly exchanging time for money.

The Assets Ladder represents a parallel path of personal value creation—skills you've mastered, products you've built, audiences you've gathered, and income streams you've developed. Unlike the traditional Career Ladder, these assets remain yours regardless of organisational changes.

Is it time to create your own Assets Ladder? It's not one ladder or the other, so you can increase your chances of success by doubling your options.

When you build both ladders simultaneously, you create resilience. A corporate restructuring may knock you off the Career Ladder temporarily, but your Assets Ladder remains intact, perhaps even providing income and opportunities during the transition.

Over time, many find their Assets Ladder becomes their primary source of professional identity, income, and fulfillment. Hopefully, this book will become an important part of my career assets.

With The Assets Ladder you can outlearn and outperform others with outdated thinking and tools.

Time

The model is designed to showcase the progression of time as you move across the horizontal axis.

You can plan into the future by using the timeline, divided into periods like months or years. In this book, I used examples with three-year plans.

The further you go to the right, the further you plan into the future. Back to the left is the past.

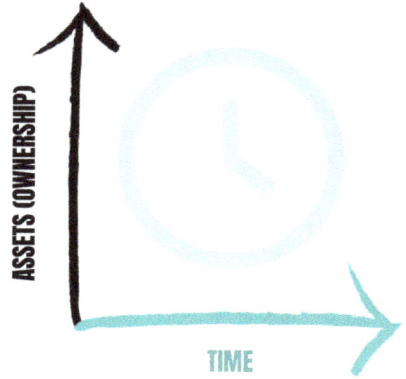

Earn with your mind, not your time.

Naval Ravikant

Assets

The Assets Ladder model is designed to show increasing ownership of assets as you move up the vertical axis.

The higher you are on the map, the greater degree of ownership you have.

Workers have 0% ownership of business assets, Partners have between 1-100% (x%), while Owners have 100% ownership of their business.

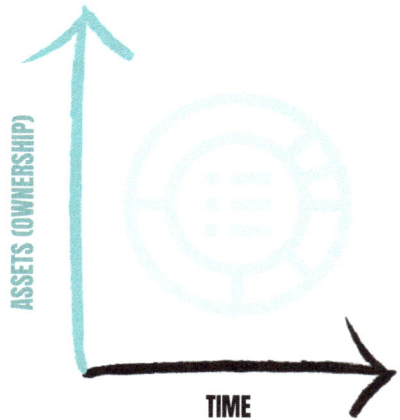

Income follows assets.

Daniel Priestley

Time is money

During your working life, how you think about and spend your time is a key determinant of success. As the biggest input is often your time, are the outputs of your time just income, or can you create some assets?

Traditional employment careers as a Worker are a great starting point for learning skills and earning a steady income. However, you will find even more opportunities for the creation of assets.

Successful career development requires a structured approach to time management and growth. A detailed career timeline is essential, including specific milestones, deadlines, and income targets.

The Assets Ladder model has a timeline so you can plan ahead into the long term. However, how you spend each hour has a big bearing on your career. Taking action today is also smart, as all delays and lost earnings are compounded over time.

Time optimisation techniques, such as carrying portable tasks for unexpected free moments and using digital tools for productivity tracking, help maximise efficiency.

All your learnings can be packaged up as Information Products for people like you. It is ideal to target people like yourself who are further back in their career journey than you are. You are the perfect person to guide them to follow in your footsteps.

The ability to learn faster than your competitors may be the only sustainable competitive advantage.

Arie de Geus

The Assets Ladder

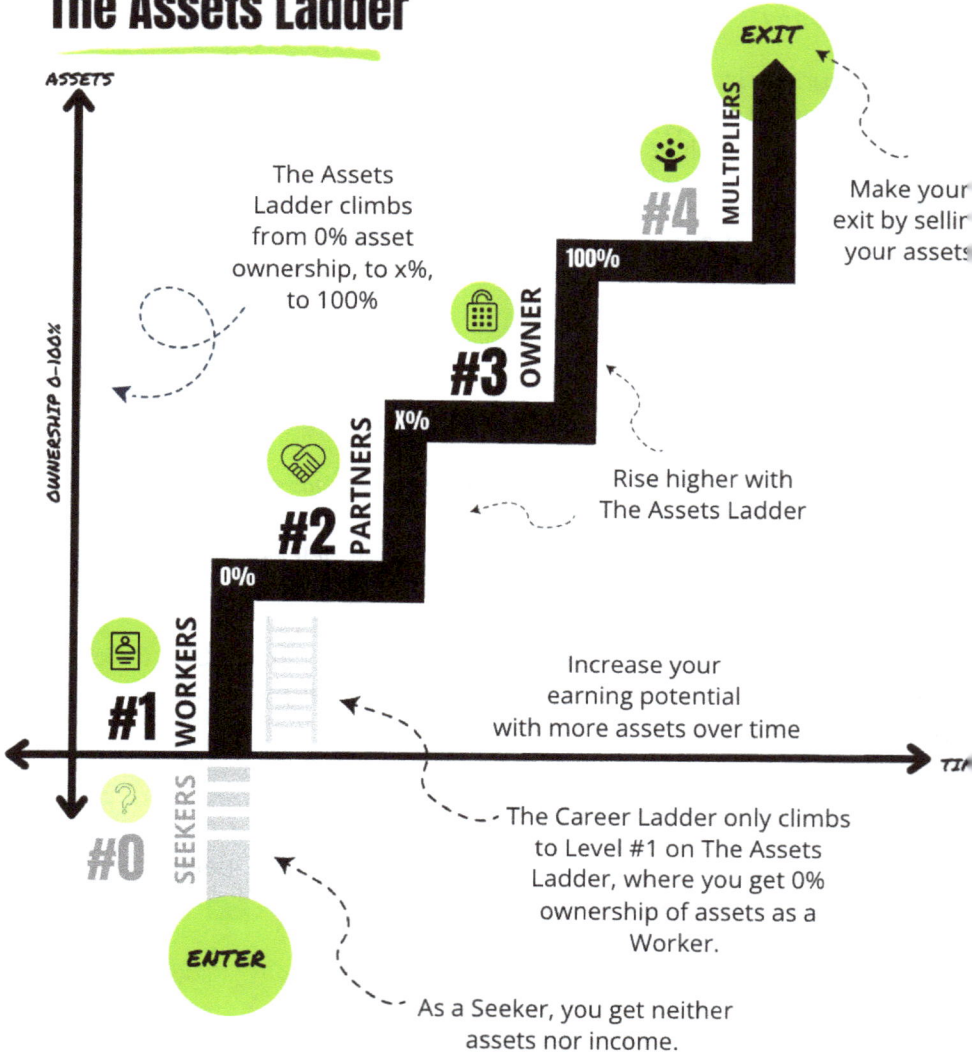

ASSETS

OWNERSHIP 0-100%

The Assets
Ladder climbs
from 0% asset
ownership, to x%,
to 100%

EXIT

MULTIPLIERS

#4

100%

OWNER

#3

X%

PARTNERS

#2

0%

WORKERS

#1

SEEKERS

#0

ENTER

Make your
exit by selling
your assets

Rise higher with
The Assets Ladder

Increase your
earning potential
with more assets over time

The Career Ladder only climbs
to Level #1 on The Assets
Ladder, where you get 0%
ownership of assets as a
Worker.

As a Seeker, you get neither
assets nor income.

TIME

If you do not have money to invest in financial assets, invest your time creating career assets.

Starting with The Assets Ladder

The Assets Ladder is designed to be a user-friendly way to visualise your current and potential career activities. While the traditional Career Ladder is shown to be useful to climb to Level #1 (Workers), you are reliant on employers for all career activities. There is no share of Assets at this level for employees.

The most common way to graduate from being a 'Seeker' is to move to 'Workers' with a new job to acquire skills, experience and connections.

Comparing the Career Ladder to The Assets Ladder

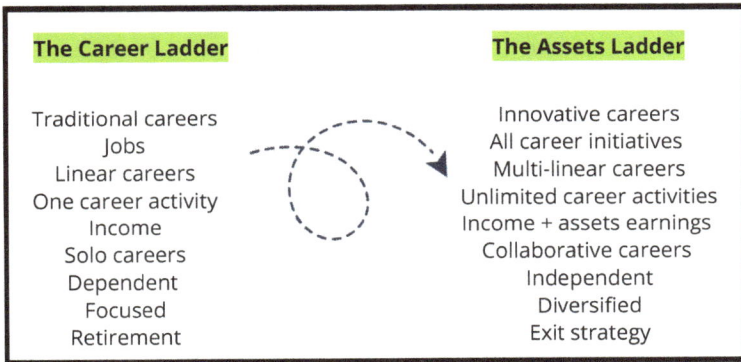

The Career Ladder	The Assets Ladder
Traditional careers	Innovative careers
Jobs	All career initiatives
Linear careers	Multi-linear careers
One career activity	Unlimited career activities
Income	Income + assets earnings
Solo careers	Collaborative careers
Dependent	Independent
Focused	Diversified
Retirement	Exit strategy

Should you swap the Career Ladder for the Assets Ladder?

How to climb The Assets Ladder

As one moves to Levels #2 (Partner) & #3 (Owner), you can start Personal or Partner Projects, either Learning or Earning. Ownership options are available for Partners and Owners.

At Level #4 (Multiplier) you can graduate to be a Multiplier, with multiple career activities. You then have the opportunity to exit or sell some of these Assets to others who are increasing their Assets.

The Assets Ladder Zones

The Assets Ladder has three Career Zones, each with 1-2 of the Career Roles: Seekers, Workers, Partners, Owners, and Multipliers. These variables are all used to personalise your career plan in my programs.

I - Profile Builders - Building skills and reputation

This zone is the entry level, where one is starting or seeking a new career, possibly without ownership. Here, we establish the foundation for career growth and search for career moves in employment.

II - Assets Builders - Creating career assets and collaborations

In this second zone, we help you search for Personal or Partner Projects that can become your career assets. Ideas can be evaluated with the IDEAS Scorecard, and earnings can be calculated with the LEAP Score.

III - Assets Multipliers - Scaling with systems and synergies

This is for people in more than one Career Role, e.g. Side Hustlers who are both Workers and Owners. The goal here is to scale up your activities and consider an Exit Strategy where you sell ownership of some assets.

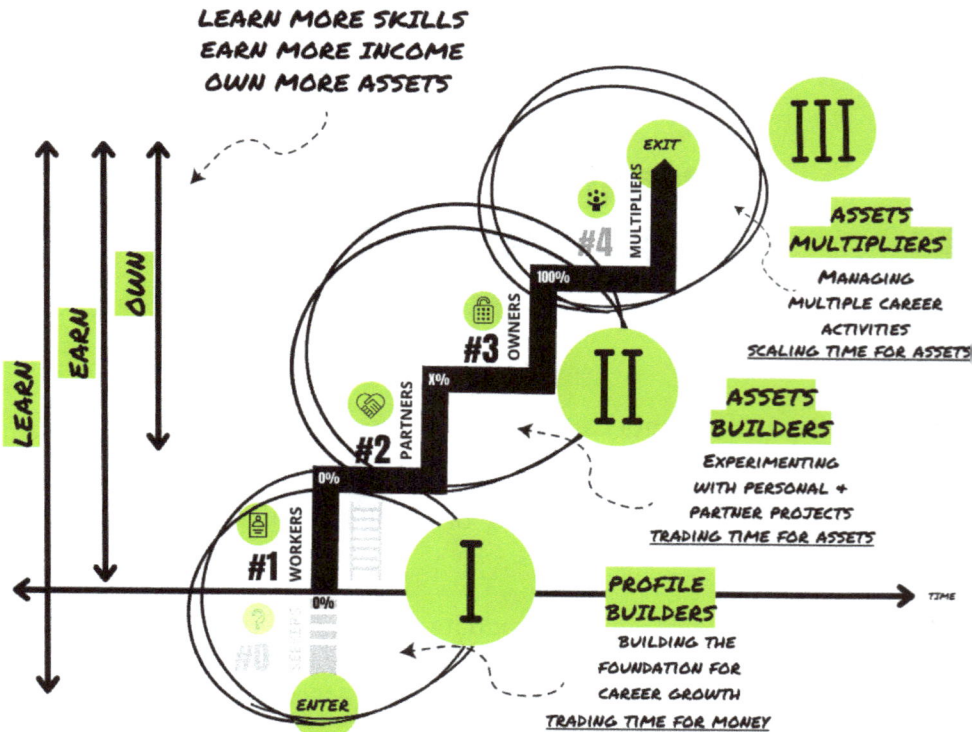

Career Ownership

Career ownership options for you over time

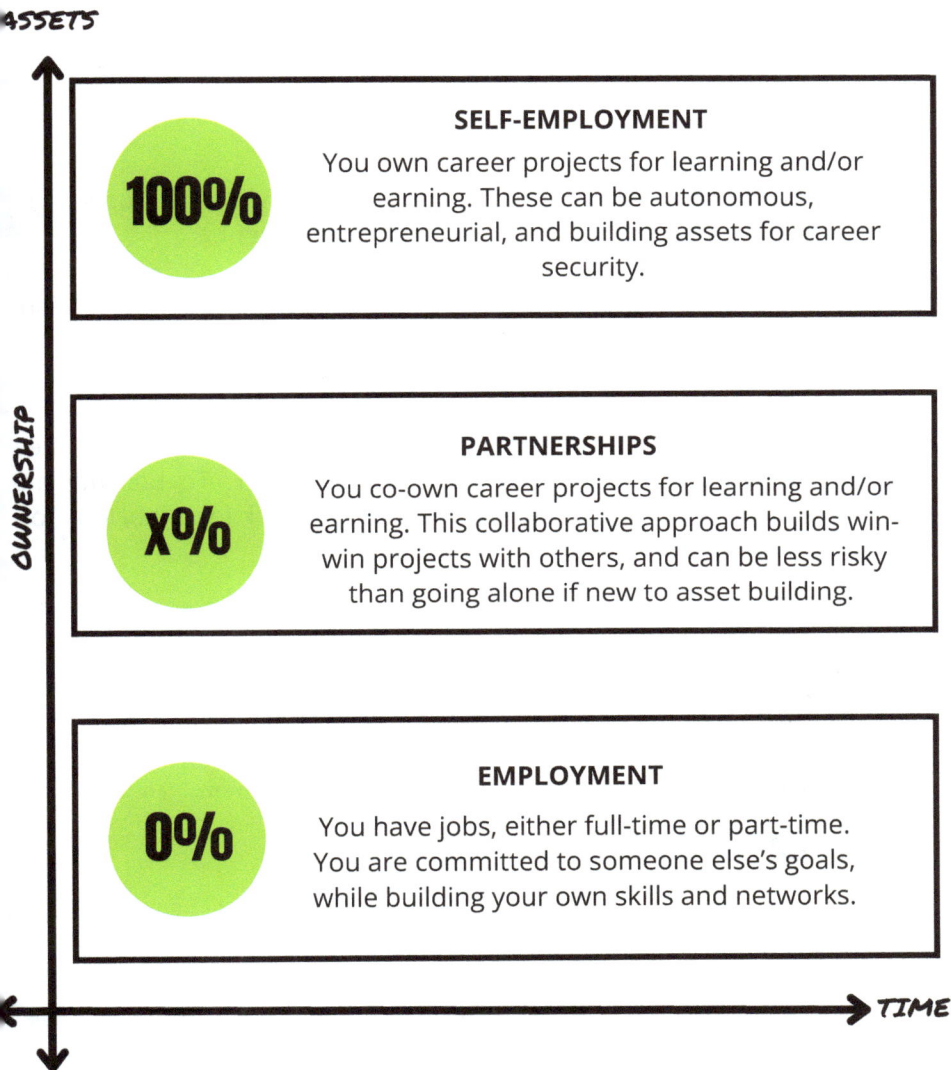

ASSETS

OWNERSHIP

100%

SELF-EMPLOYMENT
You own career projects for learning and/or earning. These can be autonomous, entrepreneurial, and building assets for career security.

X%

PARTNERSHIPS
You co-own career projects for learning and/or earning. This collaborative approach builds win-win projects with others, and can be less risky than going alone if new to asset building.

0%

EMPLOYMENT
You have jobs, either full-time or part-time. You are committed to someone else's goals, while building your own skills and networks.

TIME

There is no failing, just learning.

Employment

The ID card icon is used to denote being a worker.

Jobs (Employment)

The traditional employment model has evolved from a static, long-term commitment to a more dynamic and flexible arrangement.

Most full-time or part-time workers have no shares in the organisation that hires them. However, some Workers may get a small number of shares in a company, equating to almost 0% ownership.

Employment is a fantastic starting point to build up your experience, skills, and connections to increase your options later. To become an independent worker, follow this great advice: 'Don't look for a job, look for work'.

0%

Workers have 0% ownership of the assets that employ them.

Work for others to get the skills and confidence you require to work for yourself.

Partnerships

The handshake icon is used to denote making a deal with a partner.

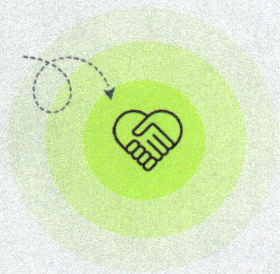

Joint Ventures (Partnerships)

As I am a big supporter of career collaborations, the next logical step in this direction is to have Partner Projects. These can have one or more partners and are joint shareholders in a project, or a business.

Shares are split between the shared owners and can vary from almost 0% to almost 100%. For most joint ventures, keep it simple but have some documented notes of roles, responsibilities, and rewards. A simple list of roles and responsibilities can be documented, and later on a Shareholder's Agreement can give comfort to partners.

Collaborative ventures are a great idea as they can tap into diverse collaborative models that leverage complementary skills, shared resources, and collective expertise.

Partners have x% shared ownership of Partner Projects, or their Joint Venture assets. An x% share can be anywhere between 1-100% approximately.

X%

Partner with others to boost your chances of success, and minimise the risk of failure.

Self-employment

The lock icon is used to denote the owner of the business.

Owners (Self-Employment)

Self-employment represents a growing trend of professionals taking control of their career paths with 'Personal Projects'. This channel includes freelancers, independent contractors, consultants, and entrepreneurs who build their professional ecosystems. It offers unprecedented flexibility, autonomy, and potential for high returns.

Owners have 100% ownership in solo Personal Projects or businesses, but may decide to bring on Partners with the offer of some shares. Either way, take ownership of your work.

Today, professionals have multiple channels to explore and leverage. To have a diversified career, it is advised to supplement employment with self-employment and partnerships. According to the World Bank, approximately 1.57 billion people, or (46.6%) of the global workforce, are self-employed. In the US, Emergent Research found that 72.2 million people are independent workers, while in the EU it was 13.7% in 2022, according to a Eurofound / Adapt report.

100%

Owners have 100% ownership of their Personal Projects, or assets.

When people are owners, they act like owners.

Simon Squibb

9. CAREER ROLES

One map, multiple roles

So now that you can see the power of building assets, you might be wondering, where in your career is the best place to do so? Let's look at career roles to see how to build that ladder.

Traditionally, careers were viewed through a narrow lens of employment. In the past, most people spent their working lives content with jobs. The key is understanding that no single approach fits all, and professionals can move around freely throughout their career journey.

The Assets Ladder empowers you to take control, offering a flexible framework for professional growth across different career stages and opportunities.

My model identifies five distinct career roles that reflect different approaches to professional growth, each representing a unique strategy for career management and personal development.

I use Career Roles to differentiate career activities: Seekers, Workers, Partners, Owners, and Multipliers.

These are dynamic, overlapping roles - most people will exhibit a mix of these at different points or in different projects. Your job is to identify your blend, then use it to design smarter personal plans.

Exiters

A final Career Role is that of the 'Exiter'. The Exiter is someone who sells their shares in career assets. At the top of this pile is someone who sells a business, and the income returns on this range from zero with 'earn outs' to billions.

Every career move should ask: 'Am I building something I could sell, or just something that pays me?' The answer determines whether you're creating assets or just earning wages."

As exits are rare, and to avoid information overload in the tables, they are omitted for now. However, always keep the exit in mind.

Career Roles Checklist → Tools & Templates chapter   53

"We are entering an era where the pendulum is swinging from the ==institution== to the ==individual==.

Dan Koe

STARTED IN WEB DESIGN, MASTERED PERSONAL BRANDING, BUILT MULTIPLE REVENUE STREAMS, NOW OWNS DIGITAL ASSETS.

Learn Earn Own

The Assets Ladder Career Roles examples.

#4 — MULTIPLIERS

	SKILLS	INCOME	ASSETS
Example: A Worker, but has a side hustle business.	Master multiple skills	Multiple income potential	Shares 100%

#3 — OWNERS

	SKILLS	INCOME	ASSETS
Example: Self-employed tradesman or business owner.	Master a craft + business	Salary / profits	Shares 100%

#2 — PARTNERS

	SKILLS	INCOME	ASSETS
Example: Partner in a project or a co-founder in a startup.	Master a craft + teamwork	Salary / shared profits	Shares x%

#1 — WORKERS

	SKILLS	INCOME	ASSETS
Example: Worker with one or more full or part-time jobs.	Master a craft	Salary or wage	Shares 0%

#0 — SEEKERS

	SKILLS	INCOME	ASSETS
Example: Student, recent graduate, or someone between jobs.	Master a craft	No income	Shares 0%

TIME >>

With The Assets Ladder, you can switch effortlessly between being an employee, a freelancer, a micropreneur and a business partner.

MARIE POULIN 🇺🇸
NOTION MASTERY

HER STORY

Marie Poulin began her career in digital design and co-founded a SaaS platform with her partner. She later launched Notion Mastery, a course on using Notion to work smarter. Today, she teaches over 1,300 students and earns around $40,000 per month.

OWNER

PARTNER

WORKER

MARIEPOULIN.COM

Career Roles Overview

Career Roles vary by the creation of skills, income and assets.

#4 — MULTIPLIERS

Multipliers - in the Zone of Leverage
- You're scaling or automating systems or outputs
- Your focus is no longer doing — it's designing and distributing.
- You think in exponential terms, seeking maximum impact with minimal input.

#3 — OWNERS

Owners - in the Zone of Ownership
- You've begun to build something: a product, a brand, a business, or a body of work.
- You're making bets, claiming space, and seeking long-term upside.
- You move from job-focused to asset-focused.

#2 — PARTNERS

Partners - in the Zone of Collaboration
- You're connecting, co-creating, or integrating your work with others.
- Partnerships, clients, or communities become your amplifiers.
- You start thinking in "we" terms — shared vision, shared gain.

#1 — WORKERS

Workers - in the Zone of Mastery
- This is about performance, professionalism, and deep skill-building.
- You're sharpening your craft, delivering value, and growing inside corporate life.
- You're climbing, but possibly feeling boxed in.

#0 — SEEKERS

Seekers - in the Zone of Discovery
- This is the stage of curiosity, reflection, and learning.
- You're searching for alignment, meaning, or your next path.
- Often marked by experimentation, reading, internal questioning.

TIME >>

#0 Seekers

Career Explorers

Many of us have had a period of time in our career when we were unemployed. While it is generally a negative experience being without an income, with a change of mindset it can be seen more positively. Why not see yourself as a career explorer?

Seekers represent a transformative phase in professional development, characterised by intentional exploration and strategic preparation. Far more positive than passive job hunters, these individuals view career transitions as opportunities for profound personal and professional growth.

They understand that periods of inactivity are opportunities for reflection, skill development, and strategic positioning. They view unemployment not as a setback but as a runway for personal and professional reinvention.

Their approach is holistic and proactive, focusing on comprehensive personal development through targeted learning projects, extensive industry research, and deliberate networking.

Seekers should invest significant energy in learning emerging market trends, identifying skill gaps, and creating personal development strategies that transform potential limitations into opportunities for advancement.

They think about organisations and markets that are growing fast and may relocate for the right career move. Psychologically, they are defined by remarkable adaptability, an unwavering growth mindset, profound resilience, and the ability to think strategically about their professional journey.

Seekers may suffer from low confidence if market engagements are mostly negative. However, with some positive thinking they can use the time for career exploration.

Build up 'career capital' by mastering rare and valuable skills

Cal Newport

This role is ideally characterised as follows:

- Actively searching for immediate career opportunities
- Focused on learning and discovering opportunities
- Actively planning future career moves
- Working on personal learning projects
- Networking and skill acquisition
- Remaining positive about career exploration

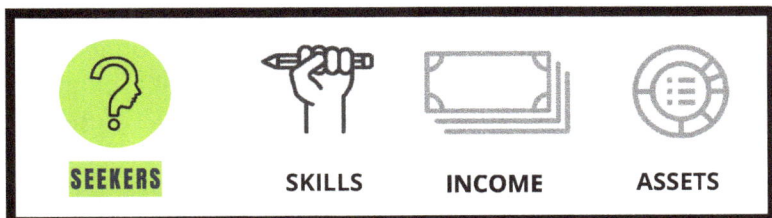

| SEEKERS | SKILLS | INCOME | ASSETS |

Core Drive: Clarity and direction

Mindset: "I want to find work that aligns with who I am."
Traits: Curious, restless, introspective, eager to learn
Strengths: Openness to possibilities, growth and learning
Challenges: May lack focus, confidence, or strategic pathfinding

#1 Workers

Employment Champions

Traditionally, most people spend most of their careers as Workers. This represents the normal employment model, contributing their skills to organisations while receiving stable income and potential benefits.

However, modern workers are encouraged to be proactive managers of their own careers, taking responsibility for their success.

You should maintain an entrepreneurial mindset, continuously evaluating your skills, market value, and potential growth opportunities within and beyond your current employment.

Make your job work for you.

Even when you're employed, you are still the boss of your career. No excuses. You can take control of your career, with responsibility for both success and failure. You can transform your prospects with a clear career plan beyond your current role.

Workers should have a commitment to organisational objectives, coupled with an equal commitment to their own goals. Workers should seek cross-departmental experiences and continuously build transferable skills.

They are performance-driven professionals who understand the importance of maintaining their market value, establishing a robust professional reputation, and preparing for potential future career transitions.

Ambitious workers should be far more active than passive employees and ideally:

- Employed by others
- Single or multiple incomes
- Stable income with salary, benefits and pension
- Proactive managers of their development
- Continuous learners of transferable skills
- Architects of their career progression

A potential downside of being employed is that it can be exhausting and leave little time for creating alternative income streams.

Nonetheless, consider creating a personal learning project for yourself, or with a partner, as a way to attain new skills you can monetise.

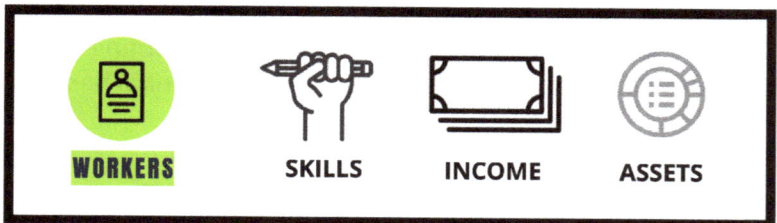

WORKERS   SKILLS   INCOME   ASSETS

Core Drive: Mastery and contribution

Mindset: "I want to perform well and advance professionally."
Traits: Dependable, disciplined, loyal, task-oriented
Strengths: Execution, reliability, domain depth
Challenges: Risk-averse, underleveraged, time-poor

#2 Partners

Collaborative Creators

Partners are people who understand the power of collective expertise, shared resources, and complementary skill integration. They create dynamic professional partnerships with friends, family, colleagues, etc. that are useful for learning or earning projects. They recognise that they leverage mutual strengths, distribute risks, and generate innovative outcomes through strategic collaboration.

Partnerships represent a sophisticated, nuanced approach to professional collaboration or solo entrepreneurship models. Some work with a Partner on personal projects before going solo.

You can share risks, responsibilities, and potential rewards with others, creating flexible professional relationships that extend beyond regular employment structures. Partnerships can range from small, two-person ventures to complex multi-party collaborations, offering a strategic alternative to solo entrepreneurship or fixed employment.

These collaborative relationships are built on foundational principles of mutual trust, aligned professional goals, and transparent communication. Partners develop flexible collaboration models ranging from short-term project partnerships to long-term business ventures, always emphasising clear ownership structures, defined contribution frameworks, and mechanisms for adaptive problem-solving.

This role is ideally characterised as follows :

- Shared ownership in ventures
- Collaborative business relationships
- Risk and reward sharing
- Complementary skill integration

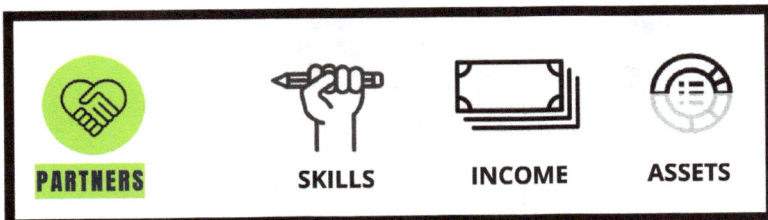

PARTNERS **SKILLS** **INCOME** **ASSETS**

One of the major weaknesses of current careers is the lack of collaboration and partnerships for mutual benefit. Perhaps buddy up with a colleague, friend or family as it's a way to de-risk ventures by making it a joint venture. Starting a project together can be a good way to figure out if you work well together, before going all in on a new business.

On the downside, partnerships don't always work out, so ensure you start small to test the working relationship with minimal risk. The success of Partners stems from their ability to create synergistic professional relationships which offer greater potential than individual efforts.

Core Drive: Connection and collaboration

Mindset: "I want to build with others who inspire me."
Traits: Communicative, generous, socially strategic
Strengths: Networking, co-creation, community-building
Challenges: Dependency, compromise, alignment risk

GREG ORLOWSKI + WILL SHU
DELIVEROO 🇬🇧

Before founding Deliveroo in 2013, Will Shu worked as an investment banker and Greg Orlowski was a software engineer. While still employed full-time, they launched what would become a global food delivery giant now valued in the billions.

PARTNERS

WORKERS

DELIVEROO.UK

#3 Owners

Independent Makers

In this book, Owners are self-employed, working on their own or with staff. They typically manage their own careers as freelancers/independent contractors, or they may have expanded their venture to hire others. This role requires a broader skill set beyond specialised expertise, demanding capabilities in marketing, finance, sales, and administration. While challenging, ownership offers unprecedented control and potential financial rewards, allowing you to fully design your work experience.

Owners represent the pinnacle of professional autonomy, embodying a comprehensive approach to career management that requires exceptional skills, strategic thinking, and strong business understanding. These people take complete responsibility for their careers, transforming their expertise into potentially sustainable businesses far beyond traditional employment constraints.

Your entrepreneurial journey demands mastery across multiple domains - from financial planning and marketing to legal and leadership. Owners must develop a robust, multifaceted skill set beyond their core career expertise, enabling them to manage complex business ecosystems effectively. They are characterised by their ability to take calculated risks, continuously learn, build career networks, and create value through innovative approaches to their work-life.

Owners must develop a holistic skill set, moving beyond specialised expertise to become multifaceted business professionals. Ownership is about taking full responsibility for your career journey. This zone is ideally characterised as follows:

- 100% ownership of business/projects
- Full responsibility and control
- Potential for multiple business ownerships
- Steeper learning curve with broader skill requirements
- Higher risk but potential unlimited rewards

OWNERS

SKILLS   **INCOME**   **ASSETS**

On the downside, being an Owner may mean you will face some steep learning curves to climb. Being an Owner involves greater flexibility and autonomy, but can be more stressful.

However, it offers a sense of personal accomplishment by creating something of your own. The greater your drive and resilience, the greater your prospects.

Core Drive: Autonomy and asset-building

Mindset: "I want to own my time, outcomes, and upside."
Traits: Entrepreneurial, bold, self-motivated
Strengths: Long-term thinking, control, experimentation
Challenges: Isolation, uncertainty, burnout risk

NIALL McGRATH

SLICEY

Niall McGrath began as a big brand Marketing Director before co-founding Fulfil Nutrition and later Cali Cali Foods. Now founder of Slicey, an air fryer–ready pizza brand, he's behind several successful food ventures backed by multi-million euro funding.

OWNER

PARTNER

WORKER

#4 Multipliers

Multi-makers

A Multiplier is someone active in more than one career activity. Multipliers represent the epitome of professional flexibility, potentially managing multiple learning projects or income streams simultaneously. Side hustles, multiple part-time roles, and diverse professional engagements characterise this role.

This might include combining employment with side hustles, managing multiple partnerships, or diversifying professional activities. By leveraging varied opportunities, they create a more resilient and dynamic career portfolio that mitigates risk and maximises professional potential.

Their approach to career management is characterised by great time management, diverse skill sets, and an extraordinary ability to transfer skills across different domains. By strategically diversifying their career activities, Multipliers de-risk their careers substantially. There may be no need to 'give up the day job', initially anyway.

They continuously optimise their time, skills, and energy across different professional streams, ensuring financial stability while maintaining personal and professional growth opportunities. Their success relies on their capacity to maintain high-performance levels across multiple domains, prevent professional burnout, and continuously evolve their skill sets to remain competitive.

Multipliers epitomise professional flexibility. While they may not have the skills they need to undertake a new activity, they have a 'growth mindset' and are willing to study new subjects.

They will also seek out people who can help them answer questions they may have in new subject areas. Making new connections is a great way to become familiar with a new field by becoming immersed in the subject.

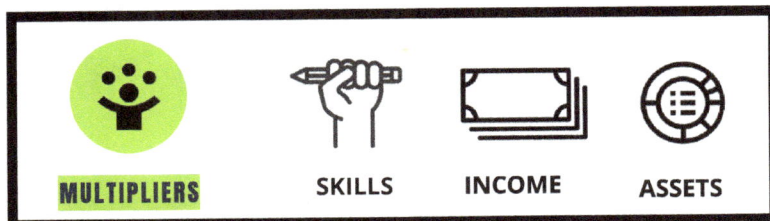

MULTIPLIERS   **SKILLS**   **INCOME**   **ASSETS**

This role is ideally characterised as follows:

- Multiple simultaneous work streams
- Diverse professional portfolios
- Flexible work arrangements
- Continuous learning and adaptation
- Examples include side hustlers

Core Drive: Leverage and exponential impact

Mindset: "I want to scale my work beyond myself."
Traits: Strategic, systems thinker, tech-enabled
Strengths: Automation, delegation, innovation
Challenges: Complexity, detachment, system fragility

AMANDA HOCKING 🇺🇸
HOCKING BOOKS

Amanda Hocking, a former care worker from Minnesota, rose to fame by self-publishing her fantasy novels — selling millions of copies on Amazon. Her remarkable success launched an international writing career.

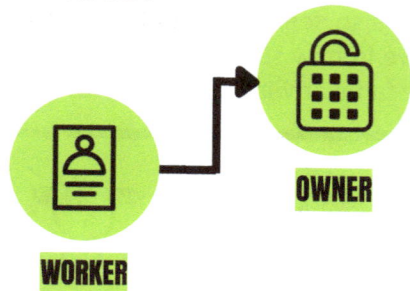

WORKER

OWNER

Characteristics

What are the characteristics of each Career Role?

#4 — MULTIPLIERS

Core Driver: Leverage and exponential impact

Mindset: "I want to scale my work beyond myself."
Traits: Strategic, systems thinker, tech-enabled
Strengths: Automation, scalable business models
Challenges: Complexity, detachment, system fragility

Questions
- How can I turn this into a machine?
- Can I multiply this with media, tools, or teams?
- How do I shift from doing to designing?

#3 — OWNERS

Core Driver: Autonomy and asset-building

Mindset: "I want to own my time, outcomes, and upside."
Traits: Entrepreneurial, bold, self-motivated
Strengths: Long-term thinking, control, experimentation
Challenges: Isolation, uncertainty, burnout risk

Questions
- How do I start something of my own?
- What assets am I building this year?
- How do I protect my downside?

#2 — PARTNERS

Core Driver: Connection and collaboration

Mindset: "I want to build with others who inspire me."
Traits: Communicative, generous, socially strategic
Strengths: Networking, co-creation, community-building
Challenges: Dependency, compromise, alignment risk

Questions
- Who could I build this with?
- How do I pitch to people to collaborate?
- What can we create together?

#1 — WORKERS

Core Driver: Mastery and contribution

Mindset: "I want to perform well and advance professionally."
Traits: Dependable, disciplined, loyal, task-oriented
Strengths: Execution, reliability, domain depth
Challenges: Risk-averse, may lack confidence and initiative

Questions
- How do I level up at work?
- Am I building skills that matter?
- Why don't I feel fulfilled despite doing well?

#0 — SEEKERS

Core Drive: Income and direction

Mindset: "I want to find work that aligns with who I am."
Traits: Curious, restless, introspective, eager to learn
Strengths: Openness to possibilities, growth and learning
Challenges: May lack focus, confidence, or strategic path.

Questions
- What do I actually want?
- What else is possible for me?
- What will get me started?

TIME >>

"

That's why the most essential trai among successfu entrepreneurs isn' intelligence – it's grit.

SARAH CHRISP

wholesaleted.com

Entrepreneur / Create / Educator

STARTED IN RETAIL, SPECIALISED IN E-COMMERCE, BUILT WHOLESALE TED, NOW OWNS DIGITAL EDUCATION BRANDS.

10. CAREER STRATEGY

Your career strategy will determine your lifetime success

Strategy is a much overused and misused word. Many mistake strategy for tactics so let's clarify what is meant by 'career strategy'.

"Good Strategy, Bad Strategy" by Richard P. Rumelt is a seminal work distinguishing between effective and ineffective strategic approaches.

Here's a breakdown of the key concepts:

- Diagnosis: Identifies the core challenge or problem.
- Guiding Policy (Choice): Decide the strategic direction you will take, and directions you will decline.
- Coherent Action: Determines the specific actions needed to address the challenge, focusing resources and efforts.

Essentially you must use your limited resources like time and money, to pursue unlimited options.

The Assets Ladder helps you see the big picture of personal strategy for your working life while also helping you identify the tactical actions you must take to achieve success. As a result, we start with the vision and also include the small details that make up the final plan.

Your career strategy can be broken down into a hierarchical framework that starts with high-level strategy and flows down to specific tactical moves. This framework helps you map out your journey from your current position to your desired future situation.

Strategy sits at the top of this hierarchy, defining the overall direction and long-term goals. It establishes what you're trying to achieve and why, considering important factors like your career stage, life stage, family considerations, personal life, personality type, and work preferences.

A well-thought-out strategy provides the foundation for all other elements of personal development. For example your strategy could be 'Diversify to Multiply' which is short for career success through diversification of income streams.

Why a career plan is important

A career plan helps you set and achieve your career goals, more than anything else. It provides a roadmap for your career development and helps you take action to achieve your desired outcomes.

You need a career action plan as it provides focus and direction for better decision-making and can help you increase motivation by tracking progress. No matter what your destination, your career journey will be faster and smoother, and less stressful, if you have a plan in place.

While researching for this book, I noted that they were very much focused on employment and not keeping up with the times. I started sketching ideas on the perfect career plan for someone like me.

A career plan is a long-term and aspirational view of your future work life. It refers to the desired end-state that you want to achieve in your career over time, usually spanning several years or even decades.

They are essential blueprints for career advancement. They provide a structured framework, guiding you toward the big picture of your career aspirations with clarity and purpose.

Whether pursuing a promotion, career change, or skill enhancement, these plans break down complex goals into manageable steps, fostering focus and accountability.

Key components include defining objectives, setting timelines, and tracking progress. By establishing clear milestones, you can monitor your advancement, adapt strategies as needed, and celebrate successes along the journey.

This exploration delves into the critical role of action plans in career development, offering insights into how you can leverage them to navigate your professional paths effectively in today's competitive job market.

There are many versions of you, and they are all right.

Bill Burnett & Dave Evans

> **Money isn't the goal. The goal is to work when you want, where you want, and on what you want.**

CODIE SANCHEZ

codiesanchez.com

Entrepreneur / Investor / Creator

Started in finance, mastered acquisitions, built Contrarian Thinking, now owns a portfolio of assets.

Source : Codie Sanchez

Who's your career strategist?

It's time for a change. A change in strategy. A change in approach to all aspects of careers. It's time to realise that things have changed completely and you need to change with the times, or fall behind.

As careers get more complex, are you going to hope things will work out blindly, or will you outsource the problem to a paid professional to help you? Or will you take on the challenge of Career Design yourself?

You may recall my definition whereby Career Design is the personalised process of combining continuous learning and experimentation to multiply your work-life potential. With my help, I hope you can create, prototype, and test multiple concurrent, collaborative career activities.

Career Coach remains the dominant label, with established niches like life coaching and executive coaching. Generally, a 'Career Coach' focuses on questions without answers, but in my career work with clients, I focus on questions and answers. Being a problem solver by nature, I see myself as a 'Career Designer' rather than a Career Coach. The role of Career Designer is emerging, but it's still not mainstream yet.

Unlike traditional career counsellors or coaches, a Career Designer takes a Design Thinking approach to careers. In essence, conducting deep self-inquiry, prototyping career moves, testing experiences, and iterating for long-term fit and growth. In The Assets Ladder, the Career Coach can help manage your Career Ladder in the two roles above, namely Seekers and Workers. They only help your career at the 0% ownership level, where you serve but don't own anything.

In my career, I never engaged a Career Coach, and relied on career advice from career guidance teachers, recruiters, and mentors. With the advent of AI, I think more people like you will 'coach yourself' with DIY tools and templates like those provided in this book.

With my experience as the CEO of an international business, I had to overcome my natural aversion to 'boring' accounts. Now armed with a strong commercial acumen, I want to encourage you to also take the financials seriously, starting with your long-term financial projections for all your career activities. With these figures, you can make informed decisions. Without them, you can't.

Use AI to help you coach yourself

As someone relatively new to the world of career coaching, I arrived just in time for the greatest disruption in the sector ever. With the emergence of AI, we all have the most knowledgeable coach at our fingertips, if we know how to tap into it fully. In the following chapters, I provide some sample prompts to use.

Jump on your favourite AI tool and drop in the following prompts for some free career advice. In your prompt, you let your AI tool, like ChatGPT, Claude, Gemini or Grok. A prompt is an information request to AI - the better the request, the better the results. You should add to your prompts that the tool can ask your questions if missing information.

For best results, upload your CV and other relevant files before using these prompts. Add in other details relevant to the prompt not mentioned in your CV like your career goals, your interests, your likes, and dislikes. You could start your career advice session with a pre-prompt like:

"You're an experienced Career Coach, use my CV and the following extra information to advise me. To help me progress, please share relevant learning and earning experiments I can run that will not cost much time or money".

You don't need certificates and fancy qualifications to do most jobs, including coaching using AI. Practical experience trumps academic knowledge in many cases, although qualifications can help you charge a premium. When you are at the forefront of innovation like this, there is no course until someone creates the course.

It was like this in social media years ago - I was self-taught as there was no course. However, I saw the opportunity and created and sold courses under the SocialMedia.ie brand I created, and it remains an asset to this day.

The future is not a forecasting exercise; it is a design exercise - you're building it.

Joshua Cohen

Starting, growing and selling a ==side hustle personal brand business== took me 10 years. I'm on a mission to help people succeed a lot faster than I did.

Conor P. Lynch

STARTED IN DIGITAL MARKETING,
MASTERED BRAND BUILDING,
BUILT CONNECTOR, NOW OWNS
MULTIPLE CAREER ASSETS.

Learn Earn Own Strategy

I want to help you 'Multiply Your Lifetime Value' and 'Learn Earn Own' is how to do it by adding ownership of assets to your career. The Career Roles of The Assets Ladder framework and the 'Learn Earn Own' model map perfectly, whether you want to work for others, with others, or for yourself.

Your skills, or 'Zones of Mastery' are the specific expertise you have mastered. Ideally, you can master a craft and match it with in-demand skills and experience. This book includes AI Prompts to experiment and find areas of work suited to you, and increase your independence.

Your main craft should be supplemented by 'multiplier' skills like sales, marketing, or personal branding. These extra skills help you generate more income and assets with your mastery, no matter your career stage.

EARN MORE SKILLS
Acquire skills throughout your career with continuous learning

EARN MORE INCOME
Grow your income as you acquire valuable skills and experience

OWN MORE ASSETS
Create career assets as you identify market opportunities

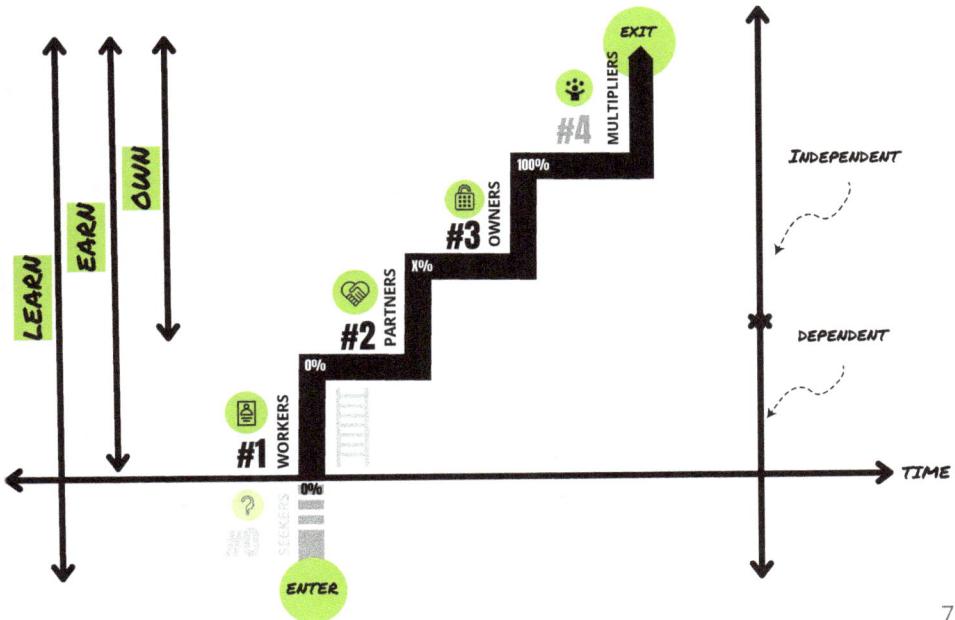

Personalised Plans

I work with my Career Design clients to create personalised plans using The Assets Ladder' framework and the 'Learn Earn Own' model.

During all Career Roles, we plan Learning Projects, and depending on their career goals, we can also add in some Earning and Owning Projects.

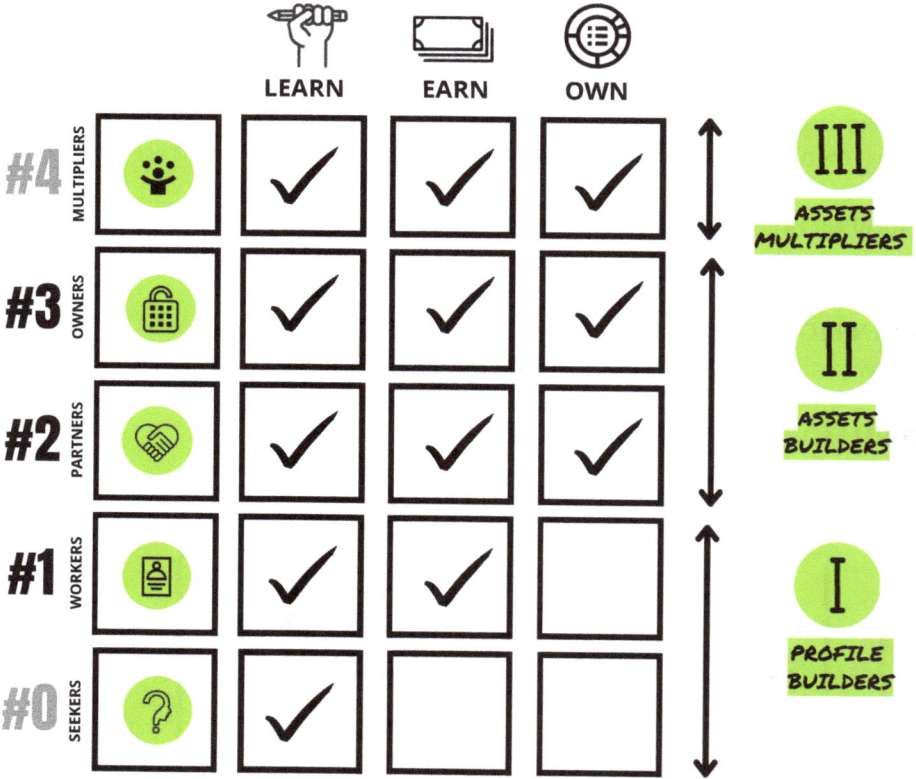

		LEARN	EARN	OWN		
#4	MULTIPLIERS	✓	✓	✓		III ASSETS MULTIPLIERS
#3	OWNERS	✓	✓	✓		II ASSETS BUILDERS
#2	PARTNERS	✓	✓	✓		
#1	WORKERS	✓	✓			I PROFILE BUILDERS
#0	SEEKERS	✓				

I'd never give my son my money – he needs to earn everything himself!

Mark Tilbury

11. LEARN. EARN. OWN.

Learn to Earn to Own,

So you are reading this book to take your career to the next level. Perhaps up a few levels. The beauty of Career Design is that when you learn how simple it is to create Learning Projects, why stop at one?

You are never too old to learn great new tricks. I strongly advise you to use 'Career Projects' as a means to create focused learning and practical experiences. A Career Project is a short, intentional initiative you run to build momentum in your career. It can either be focused on learning, earning, or owning at the outset, and evolve. Furthermore, it can be on your own as a 'Personal Project', or with a partner as a 'Partner Project'.

While it can be daunting to face a steep learning curve, join forces with friends to share knowledge and save time. Everything you learn can help your Career Projects or build up your skills for your CV. You'll learn to calculate potential outcomes, evaluate various scenarios, develop multiple income streams, and build flexible career strategies that adapt to ever-changing circumstances.

Personally, I wanted to learn about the career planning tools available for people to use. This led me to spot a gap in the career planning toolbox so I created 'Career Lab' events to test some ideas. This ended up becoming The Assets Ladder, so this book is the culmination of a series of experiments. This part of the book explores how individuals can create diverse Career Projects in today's digital world. Whether you're looking to start with a single activity or build multiple activities, the key is developing a structured approach to each opportunity.

A key lesson is to start small and begin with something manageable that won't overwhelm you, while maintaining the security of your regular job. The book is designed to make it easy for you to create and evaluate multiple activities. Why? Well, I want you to create experiments to test new career ideas.

More people will use their free time to work on asset-creation ideas. What starts off for pure learning purposes may end up as commercial success stories. You can create projects alone or with partners and change the structure as your needs change.

Career Projects become Career Assets

The fastest way to grow in today's world isn't waiting for someone else to hand you opportunities - it's by designing your own. That's where Career Projects come in. It might be a Learning Project (like writing a blog or building a prototype), an Earning Project (such as offering freelance services or running a paid workshop), or an Owning Project (like creating a course, building a tool, or publishing a book).

Unlike big career plans that can feel overwhelming, projects are manageable, time-bound, and repeatable. Each one compounds into something bigger, and together they create a portfolio of skills, income streams, and assets that make your career more resilient. Career Projects can become Career Assets. They are the building blocks of The Assets Ladder.

Now we know how you can better plan your career, we can use the 'Learn Earn Own' Model to create multiple micro-projects. Today's most successful people don't follow the conventional path. They build careers as a series of experiments, layering new skills, testing ideas, creating income streams, and gradually owning more assets. Instead of relying on promotions or employers to dictate their future, they design their own cycle of experimentation and growth. This is the essence of this book: a repeating loop of Learning Projects, Earning Projects, and Owning Projects.

After every stage, whether you're learning, earning, or owning, you loop back to start again with greater momentum. Each cycle compounds your skills, income, and assets, gradually multiplying your opportunities. The more times you repeat the cycle, the more resilient and independent your career becomes.

'Learn Earn Own' is not a one-time exercise. It's a lifelong, continuous cycle. Wherever you are today, whether you're exploring skills, monetising them, or starting to build assets, you can jump into the cycle and take your next step.

It's your life.
Make more of it.

For those with time, you can have multiple projects going at once and here are the three variations:

Learning Projects – Learn More Skills: These are intentional experiments designed to help you grow. A Learning Project might be starting a blog, building a prototype, or volunteering on a project that stretches your abilities. The goal is to create evidence of growth, not perfection.

Earning Projects – Make More Income: Here, you test whether your skills have value in the market. This could be freelancing, consulting, creating a small product, or launching a paid workshop. The goal is not just extra cash but proof that someone will pay for what you offer.

Owning Projects – Own More Assets: These are the initiatives that give you leverage. Assets, like courses, communities, intellectual property, or software, continue to generate value even when you're not actively working. Ownership shifts you from trading time for money into building compounding wealth and opportunities.

Think of a teacher: First, they learn by exploring new digital teaching methods. They earn by tutoring online or running workshops. They own by packaging lessons into a subscription service or publishing a guidebook.

Now consider a designer: First, they *learn* by creating side projects and publishing them online. Then they *earn* by freelancing for clients. Finally, they *own* by selling design templates, writing a book, or launching a course. It's a simple format - 'Learn Earn Own'. Repeat.

Here are some of the benefits of Career Projects:

- Future-proof you: Skills will determine your value in the AI age.
- Signal growth to others: Employers, clients, and collaborators respect people who learn publicly.
- Build confidence: Each project is proof that you can adapt and grow.
- Compound over time: Small projects stack up into a powerful portfolio.
- Collaborate with others: Start Partner Projects to increase your chances of success.

Learn More Skills.
Earn More Income.
Own More Assets.

> ## You can get 'good enough' at almost anything in 20 hours of focus effort. The problem is, most people spend years delaying the first hour.

ALEX HORMOZI

acquisition.com

Entrepreneur / Author / Investor

STARTED IN CONSULTING, EXCELLED AT SALES, BUILT GYM CHAINS, NOW OWNS ACQUISITION.COM

Source: Alex Hormozi 2022

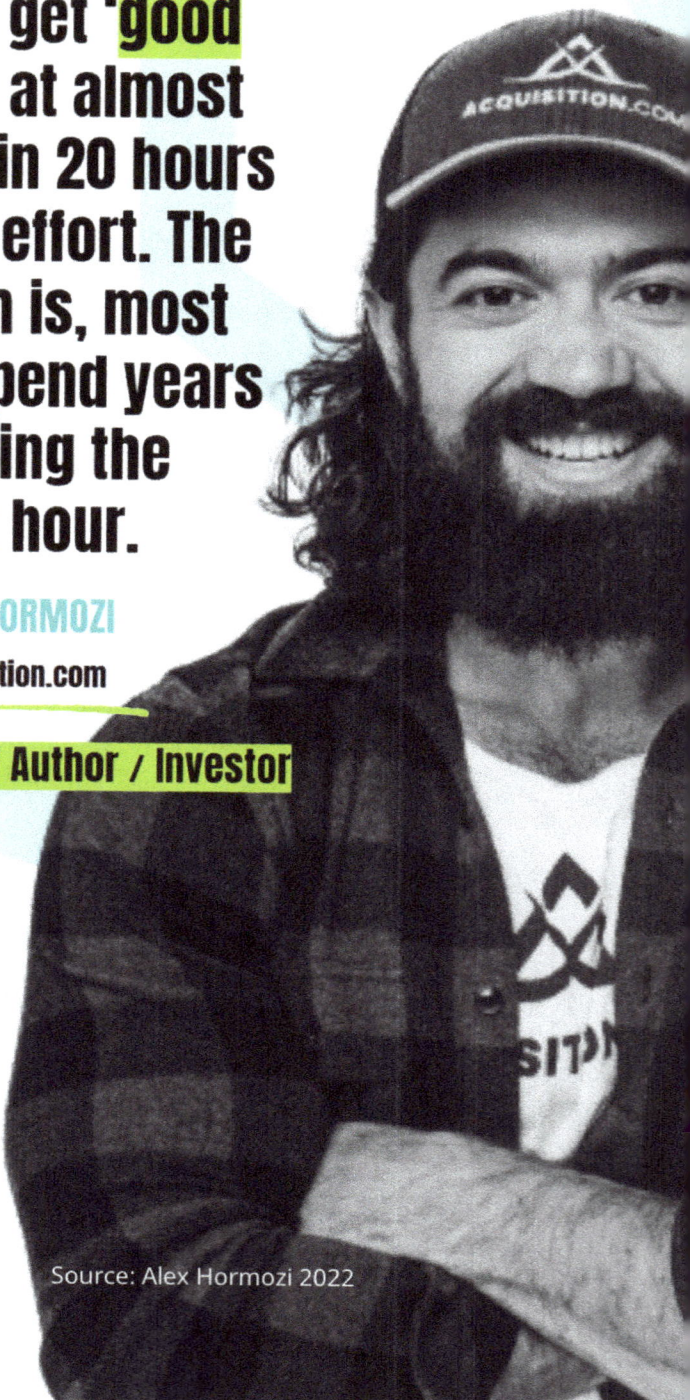

Learning Projects – Build More Skills

Your career is the sum of the skills, experiences, and relationships you gather over time. Yet most people stop learning intentionally once they leave formal education. They focus on getting through their job, ticking boxes, and collecting their salary. But in today's rapidly changing world - where industries shift overnight, AI automates entire categories of work, and career security is evaporating - learning cannot be left to chance. That's where Learning Projects come in.

A Learning Project is not just taking a course or reading a book. It's an intentional, structured experiment designed to teach you something new, while creating visible results. Think of it as 'Action Learning', a concept I learned about many years ago. You don't just consume knowledge; you build, test, and share. It's any activity where the outcome is growth, not just completion. The format doesn't matter. What matters is intention: you define what you want to learn, take action, and reflect on the results. It could be:

- Starting a blog to practice writing/building an audience.
- Designing a prototype app to explore UX and coding.
- Recording a video series to improve communication skills.
- Volunteering on a nonprofit project to learn teamwork.
- Running a weekend experiment, like a pop-up store, to learn sales.

In a traditional career, your employer controlled your learning, perhaps sending you on courses, offering promotions, or moving you to a new team. In the new world of work, you must design your own learning. Think of it this way: while others wait for permission to learn, you're running constant experiments that shape your career trajectory.

From Learning to Earning: The most powerful part of Learning Projects is that they often evolve into earning opportunities. A blog can become a newsletter. A prototype can turn into a product. A free workshop can lead to paid coaching. But even if they don't, you still win. You've gained skills, confidence, and evidence of growth. In the worst case, you've failed fast, learned, and moved on stronger. In the best case, you've created a foundation for future income streams. Learning Projects are your secret weapon. They help you stay curious, agile, and visible in a world where standing still is the biggest risk.

Earning Projects – Make More Money

Money isn't everything, but it's a powerful signal of value. When someone pays you for your skills, time, or creations, they're telling you: this matters to me. That validation is what separates a hobby from a hustle, and a side project from a career asset.

Most people are locked into a single income stream: their job. That leaves them exposed to layoffs, AI disruption, and stagnant wages. Earning Projects are the bridge to independence.

An Earning Project is any initiative that turns your skills into income. It doesn't have to replace your job right away; the goal is to prove that someone will pay for what you offer. It proves you can move beyond trading time for money. The format is flexible. What matters is that money changes hands. They let you test new income streams safely, alongside your current work, without risking everything. Examples include:

- Freelancing: design, copywriting, coaching, coding, marketing.
- Selling a product: templates, ebooks, or digital downloads.
- Teaching: offering a paid course, workshop, or mentoring.
- Consulting: helping clients solve specific problems.
- Content monetisation: starting a paid newsletter, Patreon, or YouTube channel.

The first €10, €100, or €1,000 you earn away from your job changes everything. It shifts your mindset from employee to entrepreneur. You realise: I can make money in other ways. That new identity fuels more experiments. You try new offers, build new skills, and attract new collaborators. Over time, small income streams add up. What starts as a side gig could evolve into a major revenue source - or the seed of an owned asset. Earning Projects are about more than cash:

- Proof of demand: If someone pays you, you've validated a market.
- Career independence: Even €100 a month from new sources breaks the "one salary" trap.
- Confidence & identity: Once you've been paid for your skills, you see yourself differently.
- Foundation for ownership: Most assets start as earning projects. A freelancer turns templates into a product. A coach creates a book. A consultant develops a method.

Owning Projects – Own More Assets

From Earning to Owning: The end goal of an Earning Project is not just a few extra euros. It's a transformation into Owning Projects. Freelance hours can evolve into templates. Consulting methods can become frameworks or courses. Even a small paid community can turn into a brand worth selling. Earning proves the market. Owning creates leverage. Earning Projects aren't about quitting your job tomorrow. They're about building independence, proving demand, and creating stepping stones toward assets you'll own forever.

Jobs come and go. Clients come and go. But assets stay. That's the power of Owning Projects: they create assets that continue to generate value whether you're working on them or not.

An asset can be simple, like a well-designed template that sells online, or complex, like a business or a piece of software. The common thread is that it doesn't depend on your constant presence. It grows, compounds, and can even be sold. If Learning Projects give you skills, and Earning Projects give you cash flow, then Owning Projects give you assets.

Owning Projects turn a one-time effort into ongoing returns. You build once, then benefit many times. An owned project is any initiative that produces recurring or compounding value.

Examples include:

- Digital assets: courses, books, templates, apps, SaaS.
- Media assets: YouTube channels, podcasts, blogs with ad revenue.
- Community assets: memberships, subscription groups, masterminds.
- IP assets: frameworks, methods, patents, creative works.
- Financial/physical assets: rental properties, equity stakes, investments.

Without assets, you're always starting from zero. With assets, every new project stands on the shoulders of what came before.

Learn more,
to earn more,
to own more.

Owning Projects is the ultimate career leverage because they:

- Decouple time from money: You earn even when you're not "on the clock."
- Build equity: Assets can be sold, licensed, or transferred.
- Create resilience: Assets outlast jobs, clients, and even industries.
- Compound over time: The more assets you create, the more opportunities multiply.

Owning Projects is where independence begins. They free you from trading hours for money, create lasting value, and build a foundation you can scale or even sell. The more assets you own, the stronger and more future-proof your career becomes.

EOGHAN McCABE, DES TRAYNOR, CIARÁN LEE, AND DAVID BARRETT

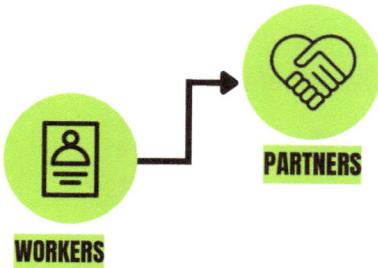

INTERCOM

WORKERS → PARTNERS

Former web consultants Eoghan McCabe, Des Traynor, Ciarán Lee, and David Barrett founded Intercom in Ireland in 2011. What began as a simple customer messaging tool has grown into a global SaaS platform valued at over $1 billion.

INTERCOM.COM

12. CAREER EXPERIMENTS

Create your own career experiments

Career experiments are indispensable activities in the journey of professional development. They offer a structured method for you to explore potential career paths, address skill gaps, and nurture personal growth.

These experiments serve as vital tools for you to try new ideas in your self-development. They offer a structured approach to exploring potential career paths, filling skill gaps, and fostering personal growth. These experiments typically involve defining specific career goals, planning activities, and analysing the results.

Through career experiments, you gain valuable insights into your aspirations, skill development needs, and strategic paths. They provide a methodical framework for formulating and validating hypotheses about your career trajectory, helping you assess the alignment between your desired roles and personal potential.

Furthermore, these initiatives offer you a chance to stand out in competitive markets, connect with influential decision-makers, and develop relevant skills essential for career success. Ultimately, career experiments empower you to make informed decisions, navigate career complexities, and pursue rewarding and impactful careers.

I've built my career on career experiments, like learning social media, video production, events, and eCommerce.

Test out career prototypes

Career prototyping, drawing from Design Thinking and product development, emphasises experimentation and iteration for crafting a fulfilling career. It involves creating mock-up versions of different career paths to explore roles, industries, and preferences. A mock-up is a model or replica of something, typically made for demonstration, teaching, or testing purposes.

Prototype your new life today.

By treating conversations and experiences like internships and interviews as prototypes, you gain immersive learning and firsthand insights. This approach mitigates risk and uncertainty by allowing the testing of pathways on a smaller scale, informing future decisions. It fosters a mindset of continuous learning, crucial in today's dynamic job market.

Additionally, career prototyping promotes resilience and flexibility, preparing you to adapt to unexpected transitions and challenges.

By embracing curiosity and open-mindedness, you can design a career path that aligns with your passions and values, promoting self-discovery and fulfillment in your career journey.

INDRA NOOYI

Indra Nooyi joined PepsiCo in 1994, first leading corporate strategy before becoming CEO in 2006. She drove major acquisitions, restructured operations, and doubled the company's profits. Today, she remains one of the world's most powerful women in business.

WORKER

OWNER

INDRANOOYI.COM

99% of people don't have a long-term ==career plan==, so they are relying on luck, not design.

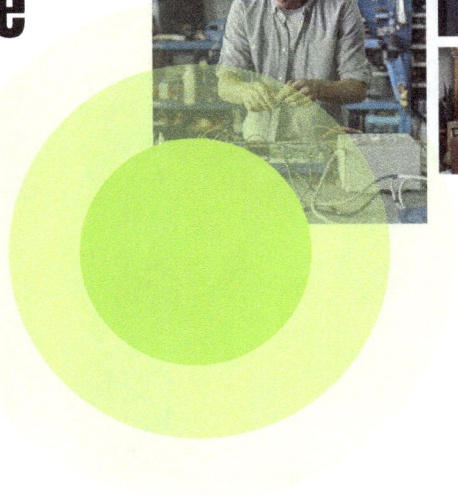

Career prototype benefits

By having a curious open-minded approach to exploring your work life and running experiments, you can gain insights and practical knowledge on your self-discovery journey.

The benefits of career protyping include:

- Designing a career path aligned with passions and values.
- Mitigating risk and uncertainty through testing pathways on a smaller scale.
- Using experiences to inform and guide future career decisions.
- Developing resilience and flexibility to navigate unexpected transitions and challenges.
- Preparing you for uncertainties in your professional journey.

RACHEL CARRELL 🇬🇧

KORU KIDS

During her maternity leave from an executive role, she launched a childcare platform. Today, the company employs hundreds and has secured millions in funding.

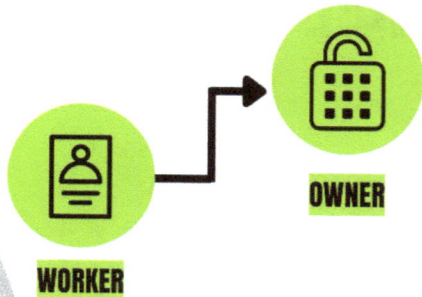

WORKER → OWNER

KORUKIDS.CO.UK

Use experiments not to think big, but to think small. What is the smallest thing you can do to test ideas and assumptions? You don't need to take over the world, you just need to make the first step.

AI Prompts [AI]

As I want this book to be as practical as possible, you can use AI for idea generation, evaluation, and action. Later I will share some free AI prompts for the following career stages:

- SELF-DISCOVERY
- JOB SEARCH
- GETTING PROMOTED
- CHANGING ROLES
- FIND NEW PARTNER PROJECTS
- CREATING NEW LEARNING PROJECTS
- CREATING NEW EARNING PROJECTS
- CREATING NEW OWNING PROJECTS
- SYNERGIES AS A MULTIPLIER

Use experiments not to think big, but to think small.

SELF-DISCOVERY AI

A critical first step before you start planning career experiments and projects is to spend time researching your 'Zone of Mastery'. In my humble opinion, you need to pick some zones of mastery from the universe of possibilities, as all the plans will flow from this activity.

Find my strengths

"Based on my CV and other files submitted, my goals [insert goals], and my interests [insert interests], what patterns or strengths stand out that suggest where I've consistently performed well or added unique value?"

Zone of Mastery discovery

"What are the overlapping areas between what I'm good at, what I enjoy [insert work preferences], and market demand? What zone of mastery emerges from that intersection?"

Strategic relevance check

"Based on my existing skills and interests, what domains are becoming more valuable in the next 5–10 years where I can build a career advantage?"

NOTES

CREATING NEW LEARNING PROJECTS [AI]

Before you can grow your career options, you need to keep expanding your skills and knowledge. Learning projects give you structured ways to experiment, explore, and educate yourself without major risk. Think of them as small bets that build confidence and open doors.

Desirability: Personalise Learning Project ideas based on my profile
"Based on my CV/resume and my current role as a [insert job title], and my interests [list your interests], what are the top 3 skills I should develop in the next 12 months to stay competitive in the age of AI?"

Feasibility: Generate Learning Projects suitable for me
"Based on my profile, can you suggest 5 practical 'Learning Projects' I could complete in under 90 days to improve my skills, with visible outputs I can showcase."

Viability: Prioritise and plan the best opportunity
"Considering market demand, personal fit, and earning potential, which of these ideas should I prioritise, and why? Design a 90-day learning roadmap for me, including free/low-cost resources, small projects, and public ways I can share my progress online."

NOTES

CREATING NEW EARNING PROJECTS [AI]

If someone is paying people for jobs you can already do, this is a good starting point. If people are asking your opinion on certain topics, this is a big clue too. You could create a Career Project to explore the potential of this as a career activity, for learning and earning.

A career only becomes resilient when you can add income streams beyond your main job. Earning projects let you test ways to generate revenue from your skills, passions, or ideas. These projects may start small but can grow.

Desirability: Personalise Earning Project ideas based on my profile
"Based on my CV/resume and my current role as a [insert job title], and my interests [list your interests], suggest three business ideas that combine my strengths and passions."

Feasibility: Generate Earning Projects suitable for my capabilities
"Based on my profile, suggest 5 practical 'Earning Projects' I could complete in under 90 days to improve my skills, with visible outputs I can showcase."

Viability: Generate money-making ideas based on my profile
"Considering market demand, personal fit, and earning potential, create a detailed 12-month action plan for the strongest ideas. Also, help me write an irresistible offer pitch for my most promising income idea, including who it's for, the problem it solves, and why I'm credible."

NOTES

CREATING NEW OWNING PROJECTS [AI]

The real wealth in careers comes not from trading time for money, but from owning assets that keep working for you. Owning projects is about building something once, like content, IP, products, or equity, that compounds value over time. They are your ticket to financial independence and long-term impact.

Desirability: Personalise Owning Project ideas based on my profile
"Based on my CV/resume and my current role as a [insert job title], and my interests [list your interests], suggest what existing work, knowledge, or skills I could turn into long-lasting assets (e.g., templates, guides, courses, communities)."

Feasibility: Generate Owning Projects suitable for my capabilities
"Based on my profile, and resources [insert your resources], create a 12-month roadmap for me to build 1 digital asset that can generate recurring income (e.g., online course, subscription, or SaaS tool)."

Viability: Generate money-making ideas based on my profile
"Based on my profile, if I wanted to sell or license a project in 2–3 years, predict which type of asset would have the highest potential market value and potential profit."

NOTES

> **"** **Show me an experimenter, and over the long run, I'll show you a future winner.**

SHAAN PURI

shaanpuri.com

Entrepreneur / Creator / Investor

STARTED AS A PRODUCT MANAGER, MASTERED AUDIENCE GROWTH, BUILT MY FIRST MILLION, NOW OWNS A PORTFOLIO OF ASSETS.

13. TAKE ACTION

Take action today

So taking action has never been easier, or cheaper, or faster. If you don't have a career project, you should start one today. Use The Assets Ladder as the blueprint for your career success.

Experiments are not necessarily designed to lead you away from the comfort and security of a job, they may lead you to get a better job by boosting your skills and experience. However, if you want to try something else aside from a job, remember that your job is like a paying client. They are paying you for your skills and experience, maybe not enough, so how can you maximise your earning power? We will explore this shortly.

You need to pick areas where you build deep skills, long-term credibility, and become known as a go-to expert, like 'graphic design', digital marketing', or 'attic conversions', etc. Before you decide where to put the proverbial career ladder, you need to do some prep work. You need to ensure you are climbing in the right location and climbing the right ladder.

You may not be limited to just one area of mastery. If you have more than one that is unrelated, you can run some experiments to see which are the best opportunities for you in the short and long term. Yes, of course, you can jump on every side hustle fad you see on YouTube from some digital nomadic guy posing on a beach or in a rented private jet. Or you can increase your chances of success with a more systematic approach to choosing where to invest your time.

Rather than picking some random faddish ideas by searching 'how to make money online', I believe you should first evaluate other better options. These are more likely to be found by searching your skills, experience, knowledge, and connections. When I say skills, I don't mean qualifications, as these are rarely a requirement to do your own thing.

You don't need any qualifications. Your experience is your qualifications.

Russell Brunson

The digital revolution, especially with AI and new technologies, has democratised entrepreneurship. Today's entrepreneurs have numerous paths to explore, including freelancing and contracting work. With flexible remote working possibilities, it is easier than ever to have multiple career projects and income streams.

"A Tik Tok account, a simple blog, an online course, or a newsletter can snowball into a business empire by reaching millions, and become worth millions. No massive overhead. No bloated teams. Just you, your skills, and your audience. In today's digital economy, even modest beginnings can lead to extraordinary outcomes," according to influencer Tim Carden.

Simply having individual elements like a website, social media presence, or industry leadership doesn't automatically constitute an effective platform. True platform power comes from these elements working in harmony to maximise your visibility, understanding, and persuasive impact. What starts as a modest digital presence can exponentially grow into a significant business venture.

The key advantage of digital platforms is their ability to scale without proportional increases in resources. Unlike traditional businesses, digital ventures can reach millions of people worldwide without requiring:

- Substantial overhead costs
- Large physical infrastructure
- Complex organisational hierarchies
- Extensive staff management

Here are some examples of digital business ideas you could test:

- Freelancing (writing, designing, coding, marketing)
- Online coaching or consulting in your area of expertise
- Creating and selling online courses
- Running a blog, YouTube channel, or podcast
- Social media management for other businesses
- E-commerce selling physical or digital products
- Virtual assistance services
- Website development and/or maintenance

How might we ... ?

Traditional business ideas + online upgrade

Traditional 'bricks and mortar' businesses can still prosper, as technology cannot perform many manual jobs. So, if you can help people with offline jobs that need to be done, you can do well with limited skills. There has been a tendency for students to graduate into third-level courses, leaving skilled workers like plumbers and electricians in demand.

Here are some examples of traditional business ideas you could test with enhanced online operations:

- Personal services (fitness training, tutoring, photography)
- Handmade products sold through online marketplaces
- Local food business with delivery/online ordering
- Professional services (bookkeeping, tax prep, legal)
- Property services (cleaning, maintenance, organising)
- Pet services (walking, sitting, grooming)

DANIEL LUBETZKY
KIND SNACKS 🇺🇸 🇲🇽

Daniel Lubetzky began his entrepreneurial journey while working in corporate law and consulting, founding PeaceWorks before launching KIND Snacks in 2004. The brand, rooted in social values, grew rapidly—reaching $120 million in sales by 2014 and a $5 billion valuation by 2020.

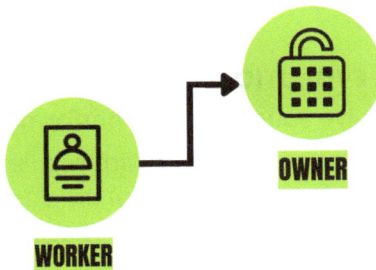

WORKER

OWNER

DANIELLUBETZKY.COM

Action Plan Overview

In this section, I want to help you with some career planning actions. The Assets Ladder fits neatly into my Multi-Careers Model as the Navigation phase. You can set the goals, the plan, the path, and the milestones. Whether you want to be employed, self-employed, or both, this is the framework for your career planning. I want to see you succeed in your career, where you have a continuous cycle of 'Learn Earn Own'.

A. DIRECTION - ESTABLISH YOUR GOALS & TIMELINE

Where are you now, and where do you want to be?

1. Write down your career goals.
2. Document all other factors influencing your career choices.
3. Set measurable targets for your activities.

B. EXPLORATION - RESEARCH YOUR POTENTIAL

Explore opportunities in line with your desired outcome.

1. Get to know yourself and your potential.
2. Research trends and emerging opportunities.
3. Build your network to find clients and collaborators.

C. NAVIGATION - MAP YOUR MOVES

Strategically plan and manage multiple career moves.

1. Identify your starting and target Career Zones & Career Roles.
2. Plan your moves, milestones, and timelines.
3. Map possible paths to get there using The Assets Ladder.

D. ACTIVATION - TEST & LEARN

Run small experiments to get real world engagement.

1. Expand your career with Career Projects.
2. Use the test and learn approach with all activities.
3. Start to build your own Career Assets immediately.

E. EVOLUTION - REVIEW YOUR PROGRESS

Evolve your goals and performance during this timeline.

1. Monitor progress with regular reviews against targets.
2. Make changes in real time and monitor the impact.
3. Measure your progress against your LEAP Score.

Test and learn.

Sample Actions

Identify your goals

To design your dream career, you need to be pointing in the right direction. Then there can be multiple different paths to get you to your desired destination.

Book Toolkit: Take the Career Assets Scorecard test and use the Self-Discovery AI prompts to help your research.

Suggestions:

- Write down your long-term and short-term career goals.
- Document your passions, purpose, and values.
- If money were no object, what would you like to do?

B. EXPLORATION - RESEARCH YOUR POTENTIAL

Research opportunities for you

Use these outputs to document lots of ideas for you to shortlist for further consideration. This research can also be shared as marketing content.

Book Toolkit: Use the IDEAS Scorecard to evaluate your ideas.

Suggestions:

- Find 3-5 ideas from trends or personal insight
- Keyword research (Ubersuggest, Google Ads Planner)
- Survey your network (Google Forms)
- Study global reports: McKinsey, LinkedIn Future of Work, OECD
- Write down frustrations, curiosities, and gaps in your industry or life
- Explore intersections of your skills, interests, and market needs
- Ask yourself: What do people ask me for help with? What do I know better than most?
- What is my Superpower?
- Start with intentional ideation based on the world around you.
- If you are open to employment opportunities, see the prompts for job seeking, promotions, and changing careers.

C. NAVIGATION - MAP YOUR MOVES

Map possible career moves

Identify your Career Zone in order to spot opportunities across all roles in The Assets Ladder in your market sector. Do you want to be dependent, independent or both?

Book Toolkit: Use The Assets Ladder map templates

Suggestions:
- Identify your Career Zone and your Career Roles.
- Can you stay in employment while looking at other options?
- Can you operate as a contractor, freelancer etc.?
- Can you identify possible partners and collaborations?
- Are there gaps in the market for products and services?

D. ACTIVATION - TEST & LEARN

Turn ideas into Career Projects

Using the 'Learn Earn Own' Model, create Career Projects on your own or with partners. Start lightweight. Learn and create simultaneously.

Book Toolkit: Use 'Learn Earn Own' AI prompts

Suggestions:
- Run a webinar to test attendance and engagement rate
- Create a lead magnet or toolkit to capture leads/emails
- Launch a niche newsletter or podcast and gauge feedback
- Use landing pages to register interest
- Survey or post for feedback
- Create a quick prototype or MVP (Minimum Viable Product)

Pitch Partner Projects: Have a career chat with a friend or invite a group of friends to workshop some ideas.

- Make the ask specific, short-term, and win-win
- Frame your project as low-risk but valuable
- Post on social media looking for collaborators

Launching a learning project. Need 1-2 collaborators (design, research). Short-term and minimal commitment required. Ready to go. DM me.

Diversify to multiply.

Build your Personal Brand as a Career Project

Share your journey and learn in public:
- Project updates, challenges, and learnings
- Behind-the-scenes stories
- Screenshots, mockups, and tools used
- Label your posts clearly and invite collaborations
- Build a narrative: show how you climb your ladder

E. EVOLUTION - REVIEW YOUR PROGRESS

Review and revise your performance against your goals regularly.

As the world of work is changing so fast, constantly review your goals and performance.

Book Toolkit: Use 'LEAP Score' calculator to evaluate your options and review your decisions.

Monthly Review:
- What did I create?
- What did I learn, earn, and own?
- Did I grow my income, skills, and network?
- What felt easy? What should I stop, start, or adjust?
- Metrics: time, leads, income, feedback
- Track your progress on The Assets Ladder
- How are my LEAP Score and Career Assets Scorecard?

No more excuses. It has never been easier. You don't need an office. You don't need a team. You don't need investment. You just need a dream.

People are so afraid of failure that they never start. Ironically, never starting is the only form of failure there is.

Justin Welsh

Some Career Projects you can try

Here are some simple ideas to get you into the experimental mindset. There is no failing, just learning.

Networking and personal interviewing techniques provide real-world perspective while prototyping and experiments can validate your ideas. Better still, run experiments with peers.

It is important to quickly test your ideas and assumptions and just get started:

- Use The Assets Ladder prompts to research all your options
- Attend events to pitch yourself to strangers
- Create a Personal Brand using Canva
- Launch your own personal brand website
- Run a meetup to test your ideas with others
- Grow your network online and offline
- Curate content on your chosen area of interest
- Create content such as videos or podcasts
- Test your ideas with some social media posts
- Create some merchandise as props or gifts
- Test time-saving automation tools
- Use AI to help you with your processes
- Print personal business cards
- Join or start an online community for your areas of interest
- Build an audience of like-minded people with an Email Newsletter or Blog
- Test selling or reselling some low-value products in online marketplaces

IDEAS Scorecard -> Tools & Templates chapter

In the following pages there are AI prompts for you to use depending on your situation.

Most career advice remains stuck in the past with the Career Ladder, overlooking the unstoppable rise of side hustles, personal brands, and going solo.

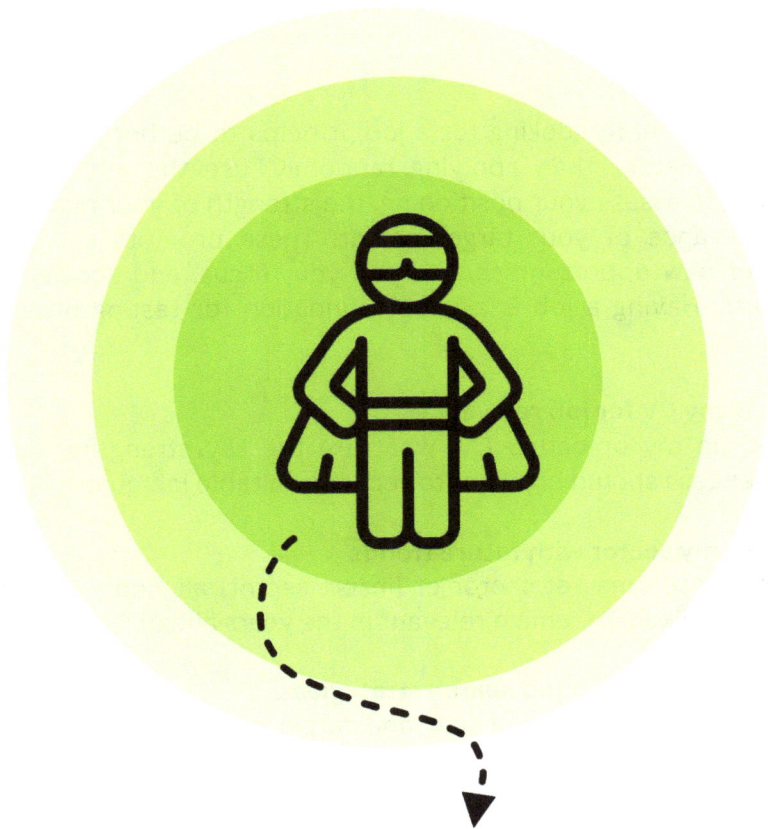

Be a superhero in your own story. What's your superpower?

JOB SEARCH [AI]

If you're currently looking for a job, it helps to be both strategic and adaptive. Rather than applying randomly, use the job search as a moment to assess your positioning, the strength of your materials, and the relevance of your target sector. These prompts can help you uncover new opportunities, sharpen your focus, and accelerate your progress. Having a job is a good foundation for testing other career activities.

Analyse my CV for job relevance
"Based on my uploaded CV, what are the key strengths, skills, and experiences I should highlight to secure a suitable job quickly?"

Validate my sector with future trends
"Is my chosen market sector of [insert sector] aligned with emerging trends and likely to remain relevant in the years ahead?"

Identify high-impact job search strategies
"Given my current skills, goals, and target sector, what are the most effective job search tactics I should use right now, including platforms, networking, and positioning tips?"

NOTES

GETTING PROMOTED [AI]

Promotion isn't just about tenure - it's about perception, performance, and positioning. Whether you're aiming to step up within your current team or move into a leadership role in your field, focusing on the right levers can accelerate your progress. These prompts will help you clarify what's needed and chart a realistic, strategic path forward. Many still want to climb the career ladder if promotion is possible, while exploring other independent opportunities.

Identify gaps for promotion
"What skills, achievements, or experiences am I currently missing that are commonly seen in people promoted from my role to the next level?"

Map a promotion plan
"What are three specific, high-impact actions I can take over the next few months to increase my chances of promotion - either within my current employment or across the industry?"

Build a personal growth strategy
"Design a 6-month plan to elevate my professional image, expand my influence, and grow my credibility within my area of expertise."

NOTES

CHANGING ROLES [AI]

If you're considering a career transition, whether into a new role, industry, or type of employer, start by exploring how your current experience can serve you in a new context. Career change is often less about starting over and more about repositioning what you already bring to the table. These prompts can help you identify meaningful and strategic opportunities for your next step. Getting a new job does not exclude you from trying other career activities as well.

Identify your transferable skills and experience
"Looking at my current CV and work history, what are my most transferable skills, and why?

Explore aligned career paths or niches
"Given my strengths, skills, and experience, which sectors or niches could I transition into where I could develop deep expertise and offer standout value?"

Design a pilot path or experiment
"What small project, contract role, or side business could I try in the next 90 days to test my fit in a new role or industry without making a full commitment?"

NOTES

SYNERGIES AS A MULTIPLIER [AI]

Today, it's increasingly common and often of strategic benefit to run multiple projects at once. You might be juggling a full-time role, a side hustle, freelance work, or collaborative ventures.

Being a Multiplier means knowing how to spot synergy, allocate your energy wisely, and make smart decisions about what to grow and what to let go. Use the prompts below to help you manage a portfolio of projects that supports your bigger career goals.

Find synergies between my career activities
"Looking at my current and planned activity, including Personal and/or Partner Projects, where are the most promising synergies that could increase results with decreased effort?"

Find, start, and optimise projects
"Based on my current skills, interests, and network, what are 1–2 new projects I could start that align with my goals, and how can I optimise or scale my existing ones?"

Create an exit strategy for underperforming projects
"Which of my current projects are underperforming, lacking potential, and what's a smart exit strategy I can apply in the next 6 months?"

NOTES

> # A **one person billion dollar company**, which would've been unimaginable without AI, and now it will happen.

SAM ALTMAN

samaltman.com

CEO / Entrepreneur / Investor

STARTED AS A DEVELOPER, MASTERED STARTUPS, MANAGED Y COMBINATOR, CEO OF OpenAI, AND OWNS A PORTFOLIO OF ASSETS.

Source: Sam Altman 2025

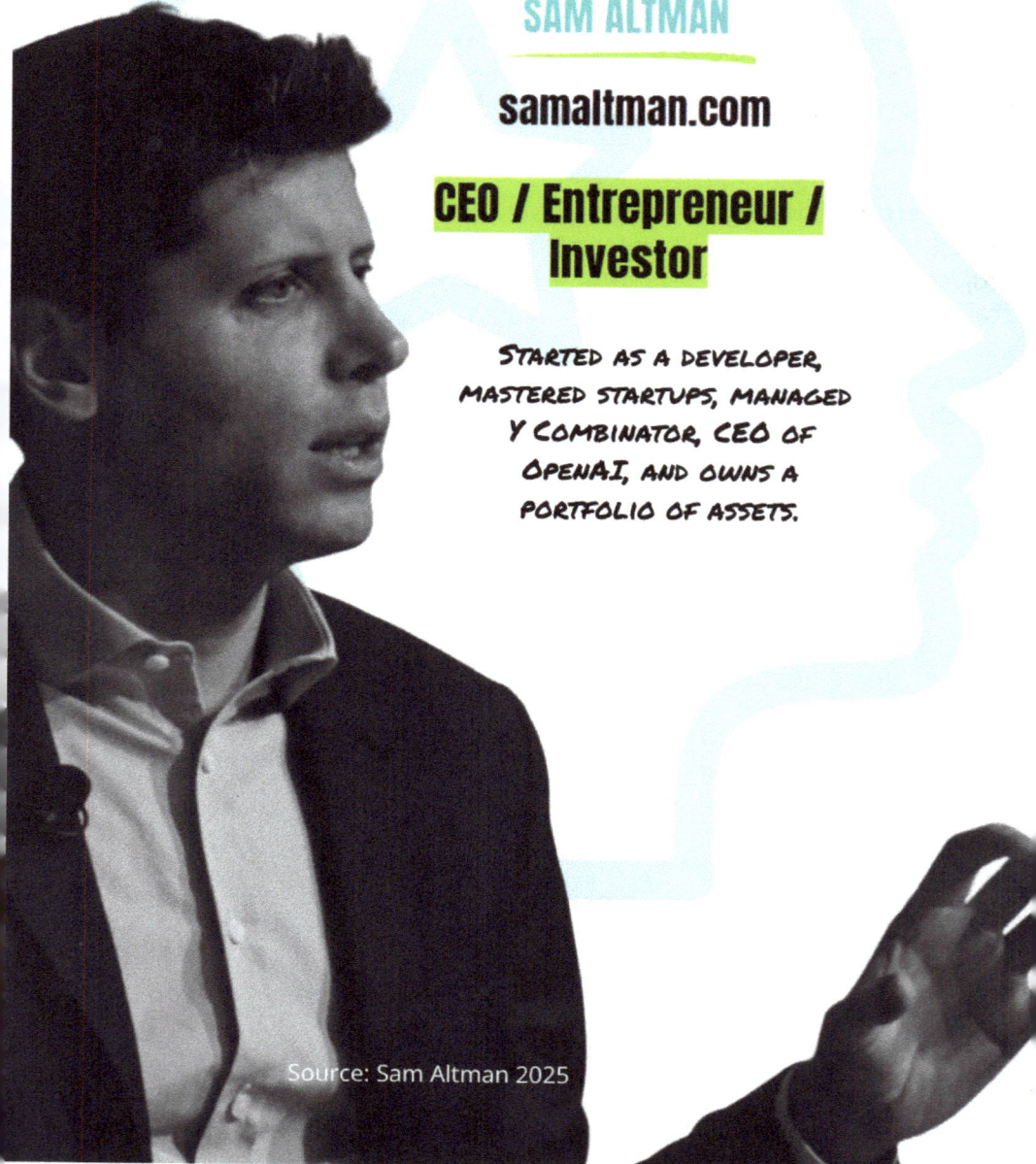

14. COLLABORATIVE CAREERS

The Evolution of Collaborative Careers

Careers have fundamentally shifted in recent years, transforming from solo journeys into collaborative multi-player games. Partnerships have emerged as a powerful approach to professional development, where individuals deliberately cultivate a network of supporters, advisors, and collaborators who contribute to mutual success.

In today's complex business environment, having strong partners isn't just beneficial – it's becoming essential for sustained professional growth and success. Partners are at the core of The Assets Ladder, and the benefits of partnerships are substantial and far-reaching:

- Diverse perspectives as individuals with different backgrounds, skills and experiences lead to a diverse range of viewpoints
- Improved decision-making involving multiple people enables collective decision-making which reduces biases and minimizes blind spots
- Enhanced user-centered design as teams gain access to a broader range of user feedback
- Increased efficiency and speed as more people are involved
- Involving potential users throughout processes increases user engagement and ownership
- Accelerated learning through peer education and diverse perspectives
- Expanded work opportunities through extended networks, often leading to hidden job markets
- Resilience during professional transitions and challenges, offering both emotional support and practical resources

Building Your Partnership Network

This collaborative approach to careers not only enhances individual success but also creates stronger professional communities built on shared knowledge and mutual support.

Skill up with personal and partner projects.

At its core, partnerships bring together diverse expertise ranging from:

- Mentors and advisors for strategic guidance
- Technical experts (developers, designers, copywriters)
- Professional service providers (accountants, lawyers)
- Industry specialists (marketers, salespeople, researchers)
- Creative professionals (videographers, photographers)

The key strength lies in this diversity, creating a robust support system that can address various work-related challenges and opportunities.

Effective Partnership Interactions

Partnerships thrive on multiple forms of interaction:

- Regular brainstorming sessions
- Skill-sharing workshops
- Knowledge exchange platforms
- Peer feedback systems
- Networking opportunities

Considerations for Partnerships

While overall, Partner Projects have many positives, some negatives to consider are:

- Reduced control and ownership
- Shared equity and revenues
- Requirements for a partnership agreement
- Unequal contribution concerns
- Complex exits if no prior agreement in place

To get started with a Partner, it can help to test out the relationship with a small project. Look for A-Players who have skills, networks and audiences you may not have currently.

A successful partnership requires clear communication, consistent engagement, and effective partner coordination. Act fast if you see any red flags.

Collaborate to accelerate.

To climb The Assets Ladder, you can avail of the opportunity to work with one or more partners on projects. There is no limit to the number of partners or partner projects you can work on, it just depends on your available time.

As the number of partners and percentage of shared ownership vary, your share (x%) can be anywhere from 1-100% approximately.

PARTNERS   X%

The Future: Collaborative Careers

Collaborative careers are the future, as careers are now a team game. You can now easily partner with anyone from anywhere. While challenges like scheduling and remote collaboration exist, these can be overcome through digital tools and well-defined rules of engagement. But don't just collaborate with anyone: collaborate with A-Players and compete with B-Players.

Three tips for building successful career partnerships

- Start small before scaling - begin with a contained "test project" to evaluate partnership compatibility before committing to larger ventures. This low-risk approach helps establish trust and working rhythms before a significant investment.
- Seek complementary skills, not mirrors - deliberately partner with people whose strengths differ from yours. The most valuable partnerships combine diverse talents, perspectives, and networks that expand your capabilities rather than duplicate them.
- Establish clear agreements early - document expectations, contributions, equity splits, and exit procedures before fully committing. These uncomfortable but essential conversations prevent the most common partnership conflicts and create a foundation for sustainable collaboration.

Being around inspiring peers is so, so valuable.
Sam Altman

FIND NEW PARTNER PROJECTS [AI]

Whether you are seeking employment or self-employment, career collaboration is the way forward. You can run some small Partner Projects with peers to accelerate your mutual career advancement.

Collaboration can open doors to shared opportunities, fresh perspectives, and accountability. By aligning with others who share your drive, or whose skills complement your own, you multiply your chances of success.

Identify possible projects and partners
What kind of collaborative project could I propose that is small, valuable, and easy to start, and what type of person might benefit from joining me in a Partner Project?

Find partners for projects
Where can I find collaborators for some of my career plans, or to partner with others on their career plans for mutual benefits of learning and earning?

Engage with partners for projects
What is the best way for me to engage with other people, with complementary skills and experiences, who may be open to career collaborations for mutual benefits of learning and earning?

NOTES

> **"My business made a big breakthrough when I identified my business partner which helped with the creation of robust products.**

DERVAL O'ROURKE

derval.ie

Author / Entrepreneur / Olympian

STARTED IN ATHLETICS, EXCELLED AT FITNESS AND HEALTH, BUILT DERVAL.IE, NOW OWNS A WELLNESS PLATFORM.

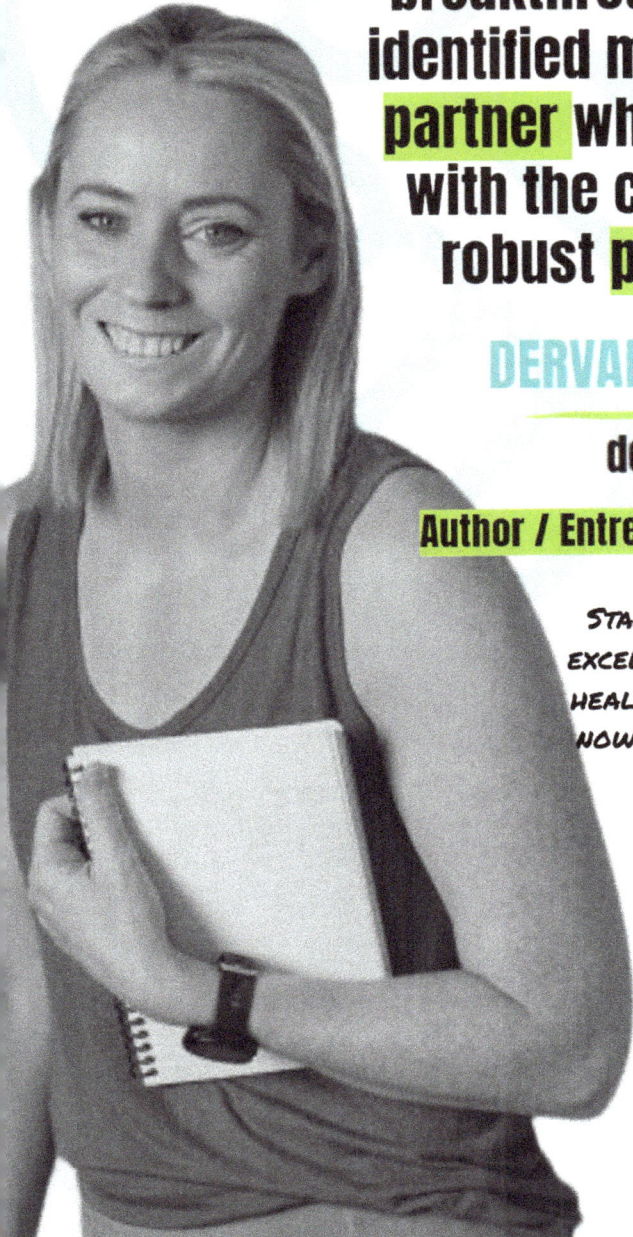

Career Coach or Career Designer?

A Career Designer can help you with all aspects of a modern career like planning and creating assets, on your own or with collaborators (Partners, Owners, Multipliers).

As an experienced Career Designer, I can help you with all five Career Roles in The Assets Ladder. Meanwhile, a Career Coach can help you, whether you are an employee (Workers & Seekers), with 0% ownership of your career activities.

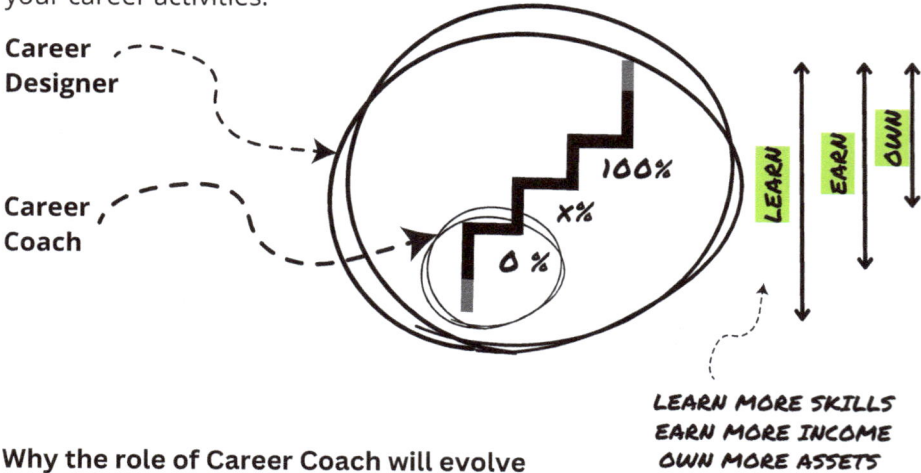

Career Designer

Career Coach

100%

x%

0%

LEARN

EARN

OWN

LEARN MORE SKILLS
EARN MORE INCOME
OWN MORE ASSETS

Why the role of Career Coach will evolve

If you are looking for advice from others, it is best to get advice from people who have taken the path you would like to take. Or at least they are trained up in relevant methodologies like Career Design.

Future-of-work dynamics: As the world of work becomes more fluid - gig economies, remote roles, AI-driven disruptions - workers need flexible, proactive career design skills, not just reactive coaching.

Demand for personalised, values-driven careers: People increasingly seek purpose and alignment in their careers. The Career Designer model supports self-reflection, experimentation, and designing work that's deeply meaningful.

Rise of portfolio and non-linear careers: For those juggling multiple career activities like multi-hyphenates and polyworkers, conventional career coaching may fall short. The same applies to creative professionals and entrepreneurs, as they require a designer mindset for idea generation, rapid prototyping, and reflection.

15. CAREER MOVES

Multiply your moves and your options

The Assets Ladder model is flexible for all career stages, helping you plan your career from start to finish. At the start, you seek a job or a career, and later you may want to start creating your own assets on your own or with partners.

In this chapter, I will look in detail at some of the pivotal moves in all our careers, when we take the leap and move outside our comfort zone.

I will introduce you to four examples at different career stages. Here's how their Career Portfolios look like on The Assets Ladder.

Goal: Owner **ASSETS MULTIPLIERS**
Own Personal Projects
Example: Alex - Writer

Goal: Partner **ASSETS BUILDERS**
Co-own Partner Projects
Example: Rohan - Developer

Goal: Climber **PROFILE BUILDERS**
Climb the Career Ladder
Example: Ben - Videographer

Goal: Launcher **ASSETS BUILDERS**
Launch your career
Example: Clare - Graphic Designer

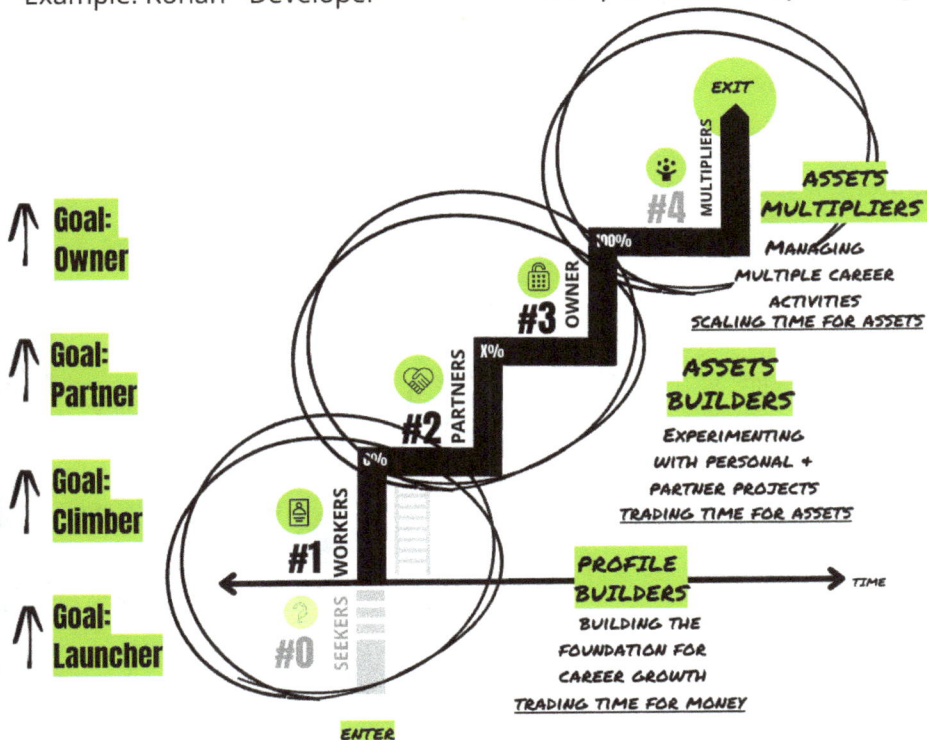

Goal: Owner

Goal: Partner

Goal: Climber

Goal: Launcher

EXIT

MULTIPLIERS

#4

100%

ASSETS MULTIPLIERS
MANAGING MULTIPLE CAREER ACTIVITIES
SCALING TIME FOR ASSETS

#3 OWNER

X%

#2 PARTNERS

ASSETS BUILDERS
EXPERIMENTING WITH PERSONAL + PARTNER PROJECTS
TRADING TIME FOR ASSETS

0%

#1 WORKERS

SEEKERS

#0

PROFILE BUILDERS
BUILDING THE FOUNDATION FOR CAREER GROWTH
TRADING TIME FOR MONEY

TIME

ENTER

Getting started with The Assets Ladder

The Assets Ladder comes to life as a map for ambitious people trying to multiply their career options, to multiply their potential. Unlike the career ladder, which is one rung at a time, one person at a time, with my new model, you can have multiple career activities in multiple rows, giving you unlimited potential.

While the duration of your career plan timeline is up to you, I recommend using a three-year timeline so you have time to make big career moves. However, I also help clients with shorter timelines like 30, 60, or 90-day sprints for faster career transitions.

Start: Join the map in the role(s) you are currently in, drawing a square for an earning project, or a circle for a learning project. If you are starting your career as a 'Seeker', think about what you can learn while you earn.

Milestones: You can track actions or milestones along your journey, almost like a trail of breadcrumbs leading you to your goals. Beneficial actions can include acquiring new skills or finding partners.

Moves: Think about your next move towards your desired outcome or end destination. All career stages and moves are not limited to one option, as you can have multiple options here too.

Exit: If you own assets you want to sell, then this is planning a career exit strategy. If you have no assets, then you just retire like regular workers.

Below are some icons used in The Assets Ladder planning and group workshops.

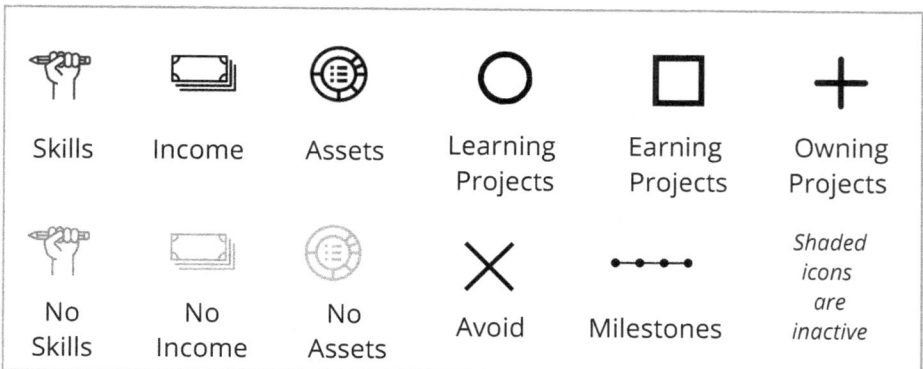

Skills	Income	Assets	Learning Projects	Earning Projects	Owning Projects
No Skills	No Income	No Assets	Avoid	Milestones	*Shaded icons are inactive*

Goal: Launcher

Clare

Graphic Designer
London

CAREER PATH

1. New Job
2. Promotion
3. Ends Job
4. New Partnership

LEARN: Clare is starting her career and wants the stability of employment.

EARN: She starts a job as a graphic designer, and continues to learn her craft on the job and with micro-qualifications.

OWN: Ultimately she wants to quit this job and find a business partner to co-create and co-own a new business.

WPO = WORKERS PARTNERS OWNERS

		2026			2027			2028		
		W	P	O	W	P	O	W	P	O
MULTIPLIERS	SKILLS	✊			✊	✊		✊	✊	
	INCOME	💵			💵	💵		💵	💵	
	ASSETS	◉			◉	◉		◉	◉	

#4 MULTIPLIERS

#3 OWNERS

#2 PARTNERS — EXTEND

#1 WORKERS

#0 SEEKERS

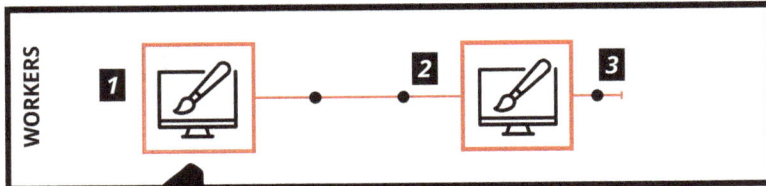
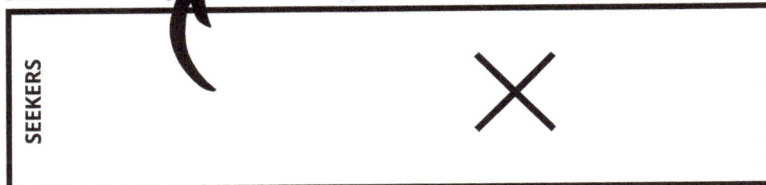

Goal: Climber

Ben

Videographer
Berlin

CAREER PATH

1. New Job
2. Promotion
3. Ends Job
4. New Job
5. New job

LEARN: Ben began his career as an employee with entry-level salary in a design agency where he gained valuable experience and built up his portfolio of work.

EARN: Ben likes the stability of employment, but is ambitious and wants to climb the ladder. He is happy to stay as a designer but would like to have two jobs as he is saving to buy a home.

OWN: He has no ownership ambitions.

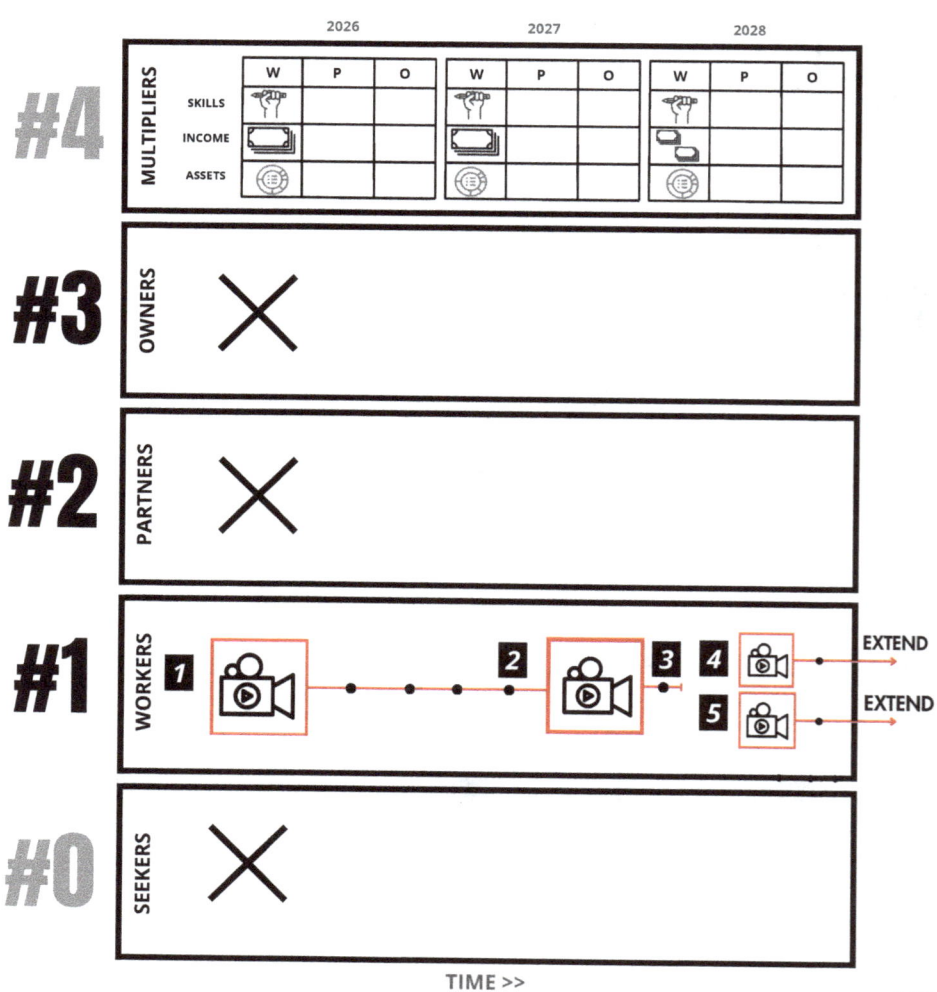

#4 MULTIPLIERS

		2026			2027			2028		
		W	P	O	W	P	O	W	P	O
SKILLS										
INCOME										
ASSETS										

#3 OWNERS ✕

#2 PARTNERS ✕

#1 WORKERS

1 ▷ ... **2** ▷ **3** **4** ▷ **EXTEND**
5 ▷ **EXTEND**

#0 SEEKERS ✕

TIME >>

Alex
Writer
Dublin

CAREER PATH

1 Job
2 Ends Job
3 New Partnership
4 Exit Partnership
5 New Personal Project
6 Exit Personal Project

LEARN: She had a job for years as a copywriter in an advertising agency.

EARN: In addition to her job, later in life she started writing short stories which she sold as books and eBooks. In a partnership she licensed her creations for shared revenue.

OWN: Alex see partnerships as core to her future career. For her exit strategy she has to consider her company IP and clients, eBook recurring revenue and Personal Brand community.

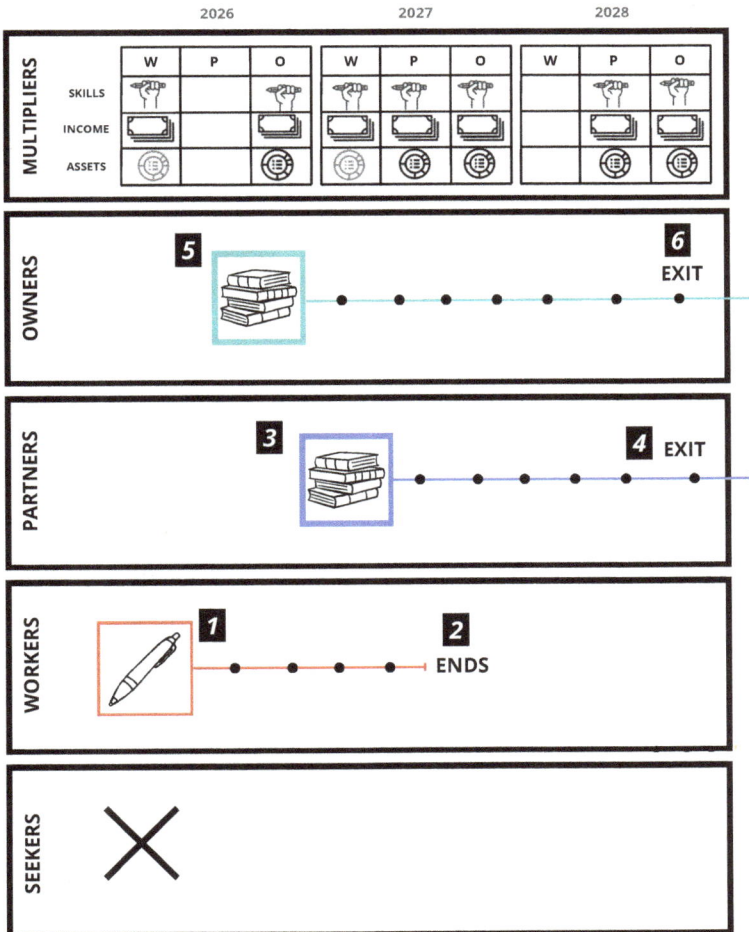

		2026			2027			2028		
MULTIPLIERS		W	P	O	W	P	O	W	P	O
	SKILLS	✊		✊	✊	✊	✊		✊	✊
	INCOME	💵		💵	💵		💵	💵		💵
	ASSETS	◉		◉	◉	◉	◉		◉	◉

#4

#3 — OWNERS — 5 ... 6 EXIT

#2 — PARTNERS — 3 ... 4 EXIT

#1 — WORKERS — 1 ... 2 ENDS

#0 — SEEKERS — ✕

TIME >>

Rohan

Developer
San Francisco

CAREER PATH

1 New Job
2 Promotion
3 Ends Job
4 New Personal Project

LEARN: He starts work as a junior developer. He decided to pursue his entrepreneurial dreams and started his own software company, while keeping his day job.

EARN: Ultimately he will quit his job when he is making enough income from his software revenues.

OWN: Rohan wants to own assets like his own software and a tech business.

TIME >>

Map your future career options

Using your research to date, I find that it helps people when their career options are mapped out on paper. Sketch three distinct plans, each of three years' duration, in The Assets Ladder map below. You don't need to know all the details; start with the big picture, and the details will emerge.

Ideally, use a separate sheet for each career path and make note of what you want to learn, earn, and own. Start where you are now, e.g. Worker in 2026, and plot your desired destination at the end of 2028.

Blank map templates are in Tools & Templates, and a hat tip to the creators of Odyssey Planning, Bill Burnett and Dave Evans at Stanford.

		2026			2027			2028		
		W	P	O	W	P	O	W	P	O
#4	**MULTIPLIERS** SKILLS									
	INCOME									
	ASSETS									
#3	**OWNERS**									
#2	**PARTNERS**									
#1	**WORKERS**									
#0	**SEEKERS**									

TIME >>

Start a Career Project with partners

DIARMUID, NIALL + KARL 🇮🇪
GYM + COFFEE

THEIR STORY

Former corporate workers, Diarmuid McSweeney, Niall Horgan, and Karl Swaine launched Gym+Coffee as a side hustle. What began as a fitness lifestyle brand is now a household name in Ireland and raised €17m to grow globally.

WORKER

OWNER

GYMPLUSCOFEE.COM

16. TOOLS & TEMPLATES

DIY

Templates
TheAssetsLadder.com

Some free tools you can try

Having the best tools for the job is critical to success, and hence, I created this new book and toolkit to fill the gap in the market.

No matter the stage of your work life, these tools can help you see the big picture and take action.

"Launching a startup or even a Minimum Viable Product (MVP) has never been more affordable. Here's a zero-cost, no-code, approach to validate a project:

- Typedream to build the landing page
- Copy.ai to produce text for landing page
- Canva to create designs
- Ideogram to generate visuals
- Figma to show mockups of your app in action
- Loom to have a founder walk through the product
- Persona to verify user identities
- Pitch to create downloadable ebooks or presentations about product
- Buffer to publish updates on social media
- Tally to create forms to collect interested users
- Notion to add internal notes and sync with Tally's forms into a database
- Beehiiv to manage mailing lists for interested early users
- Slack to manage a community of interested early users
- Luma to setup recurring meetups with your first members
- Get an awesome landing page.
- Show people what your product will look like.
- Spread the word.
- Collect early interest.
- Build them into a community.

It is that simple. And it will cost you $0".

Source: Ed Giansante 2024

We're all students.
And teachers.

Career Assets Scorecard

Evaluate your career assets - each tick is 4 points x 25 = 100 points max

1. Personal Assets / Personal Brand

Strong personal brand and/or reputation (testimonials, press)
Personal website or landing pages with regular traffic
Newsletter or mailing list
Social media profiles, connections, and content
Knowledge and repeatable practices/systems that generate value
Summary: Are new people finding and trusting your work?

2. Knowledge Assets

Frameworks, templates, or systems you've developed
Talks, workshops, or toolkits you can deliver or license
Deep expertise, original thinking, and content published
Certifications, courses, or training you've completed
Repeatable systems that create value for you and others
Summary: How reusable and monetisable is your knowledge?

3. Digital Assets

Packaged content as eBooks, paid PDFs, or guides, etc.
Online programs, courses, or email challenges
Tools/templates e.g., Notion, Canva, Excel, Figma
Applications for web or mobile, creating your own data
Content libraries, e.g., visuals, videos, podcasts, animations
Summary: Do you have assets that sell or deliver value at scale?

4. Collaborative Assets

Joint ventures or group experiments to test ideas
Equity or revenue share in projects/businesses
Long-term partnerships, co-creators, and affiliate deals
Community or audience you've helped build
Systems to delegate to teams, VAs, freelancers, or automations
Summary: Are you leveraging other people's platforms or audiences?

5. Income Streams (Active & Passive)

Trading time-for-money income and retainers
Product sales (one-off or subscription)
Audience Ad, Affiliate, or sponsorship income
Royalties or licensing for ideas and IP
Speaking or teaching in-person or online
Summary: How diversified is your career income?

Career Roles Checklist

Which Career Roles sounds most like you now? Tick the boxes.

#4 Multipliers - I'm in the Zone of Leverage
I'm focused on scaling through systems, technology and teams.
I'm moving from doing the work to designing how it grows.
I'm chasing exponential results with minimal input.
Prompt: "How can I scale myself through tools, platforms, or people?"

#3 Owners - I'm in the Zone of Ownership
I'm making bets, claiming space, and thinking about long-term upside.
I'm shifting from job-focused to asset-focused.
I've started building something of my own" a project, a brand, a business, or a body of work.
Prompt: "What asset am I building that will pay me long after I build it?"

#2 Partners - I'm in the Zone of Collaboration
I feel most energised when building with others.
I'm focused on partnerships, co-creation, and collective momentum.
I think in "we" terms, like shared vision, shared rewards.
Prompt: "Who can I build with that expands the impact and joy of this work?"

#1 Workers - I'm in the Zone of Mastery
I'm focused on performance, professionalism, and deepening my craft.
I'm delivering value and growing inside a structured system.
I'm climbing, but at times, I wonder if I'm also getting boxed in.
Prompt: "What skills am I mastering - and where could they take me next?"

#0 Seekers - I'm in the Zone of Discovery
I'm in a season of curiosity, reflection, and learning.
I'm searching for alignment, meaning, or my next path.
I spend time exploring, reading, and questioning what's next for me.
Prompt: "What could I explore that reveals more of who I am?"

Your career is your business.

Your Career Tracker

Which Career Roles can you tick for the past, present, and future?

				PAST	PRESENT	FUTURE
#4  **MULTIPLIERS** MULTI-MAKER	You have more than one career activity.	"I think about systems, leverage, and how to grow my output."		☐	☐	☐
#3  **OWNERS** INDEPENDENT MAKERS	You own career projects for learning and/or earning.	"I'm building something that I own, something of value."		☐	☐	☐
#2  **PARTNERS** COLLABORATIVE CREATORS	You co-own career projects for learning and/or earning.	"I often think in terms of partnership and collaboration, and love working with others on shared goals."		☐	☐	☐
#1  **WORKERS** EMPLOYMENT CHAMPIONS	You have jobs, either full-time or part-time.	"I'm focused on performing well and growing within my current job."		☐	☐	☐
#0  **SEEKERS** CAREER EXPLORERS	You're not working in jobs or career projects.	"I'm exploring new ideas or directions. I want clarity, purpose, and a good fit for me."		☐	☐	☐

Map your Projects

Map your current positions, and your desired outcome.

#4 MULTIPLIERS

#3 OWNERS

#2 PARTNERS

#1 WORKERS

#0 SEEKERS

TIME >>

The Assets Ladder Map

Use this map for planning potential career moves in the next three years

		2026			2027			2028		
		W	P	O	W	P	O	W	P	O
MULTIPLIERS	SKILLS									
	INCOME									
	ASSETS									

#4

#3 OWNERS

#2 PARTNERS

#1 WORKERS

#0 SEEKERS

TIME >>

Learn Earn Own

Plan your Learning, Earning, and Owning Projects

LEARN

EARN

OWN

Many **great** **ideas** sound crazy at first.

HAMDI ULUKAYA 🇺🇸/🇹🇷
CHOBANI

HIS STORY

Hamdi Ulukaya arrived in the U.S. in 1994 and started as a farmhand. In 2005, he founded Chobani after buying an abandoned yogurt plant. Within five years, it became the top U.S. brand, reaching over $1 billion in annual sales.

WORKER

OWNER

CHOBANI.COM

IDEAS Scorecard

The IDEAS Scorecard is a proprietary framework to evaluate new business ideas. Score 1–5 for each, where 1 is very weak and 5 is very strong.

I – Income Potential

What's the business model (product, service, ads, subscription, etc.)?
Are margins healthy (15%+ for physical, much higher for digital)?
Is there potential for recurring revenue or just one-off sales?
How quickly can this business become cash-flow positive?

D – Demand (Market Size & Growth)

Is there proven demand for this offering today?
How urgent is the problem this idea solves for customers?
How big is the Total Addressable Market (TAM)?
Is the market growing, stagnant or shrinking?

E – Edge (Unfair Advantage)

Do you have unique skills, networks, or assets competitors can't copy?
Does the idea create IP, branding, or authority advantages?
Are there high barriers to entry that protect you from copycats?
Do you have existing credibility or proof (audience, results, expertise)?

A – Assets Potential

Can the business grow beyond just you doing the work?
Can systems, automation, or outsourcing multiply your efforts?
Does the business model allow for exponential growth (not just linear)?
Can this eventually become an asset you own, not just a job you do?

S – Suitability (Lifestyle Fit)

Does this align with your skills, values, and interests?
Does it support your lifestyle goals (time, freedom, location, family)?
Are you happy with the relationship between the risks and rewards?
Does this idea fit with your bigger career vision e.g. The Assets Ladder?

Scoring Guide

80–100 = Excellent Idea - pursue with confidence.
60–79 = Promising Idea - refine key weaknesses before investing.
40–59 = Risky Idea - significant flaws, proceed with caution.
<40 = Poor Idea - not worth major time or money investment.

What if?

Career Tools

Free or low-cost tools for career and side business success

Tool	Use case	Why it's great
Personal Management		
Notion	Task/project/career tracking	All-in-one workspace; free for personal use
Trello	Visual task and goal management	Easy Kanban boards for tracking both job & business
Clockify	Time tracking for work/business	Free and great for seeing where your time goes
Google Calendar	Time blocking	Schedule work, business, and rest time in one place
RescueTime	Productivity insights	Analyses how you spend time on devices
Research		
StrengthsFinder / CliftonStrengths	Evaluate your strengths	Low cost personality research
16personalities.com	Look into personality types	Low cost personality research
Google Trends	Identify search trends	Based on Google data
Google Ads Planner	Check keyword usage	Based on Google data
Product Hunt	Look at new product launches	See what's voted the most popular
Courses		
Coursera	Tech, business, soft skills	Free courses from top universities (pay for certificate)
LinkedIn Learning	Career-focused skills	Often free via library card
YouTube	Business building tutorials	Millions of high-quality videos
Udemy, HubSpot Academy, Google	Business, Marketing, CRM, Sales etc.	Great for early business learning
Career Network		
LinkedIn	Networking, career tracking	Essential for visibility and opportunity discovery
Hunter.io (free tier)	Find professional email addresses	Useful for partnerships, B2B sales outreach
JobScan (free limited)	Resume optimisation	Tailors CVs to match job descriptions
Business Operations		
Stripe, PayPal	Payments for online business	Easy setup, widely accepted
Substack / Beehiiv	Newsletters & audience building	Free to start and monetise over time
Gumroad, Stan Store Ko-fi, Patreon, Skool Shopify, Kit.com	Sell product, digital products, memberships	Simple platforms with low/no upfront cost
Google Workspace (or Gmail + Drive)	Docs, sheets, email	Free (or low-cost for business email & storage)

Tool	Use case	Why it's great
Content Creation		
Notion	Use for content calendars	Get templates from other users
Canva	Design for logos, posts, pitch decks	Low cost with lots of templates
CapCut	Video editing for non-experts	Low cost and easy to use
ChatGPT, Claude, Gemini, Grok etc.	Can be used to generate ideas for social media etc.	Low cost and can provide lots of ideas to review
Experiments		
Tally.so or Google Forms	Surveys & validation	Collect user feedback, leads, or early interest
Namechk / NameCheap GoDaddy	Brand/username checker	Ensure your brand name is available across platforms
Carrd	One-page business websites	Simple, beautiful, and costs $19/year
ChatGPT	Idea validation, copywriting	Get help with business naming, research, emails
Substack, Kit.com, Beehiiv	Content and email newsletter monetisation platforms	Adopt these tools and join their communities of creators
Streamlabs, Streamyard	Broadcast live shows online	Low cost powerful suite of tools
Lovable, Replit, V0, Claude, Codex	Create prompt-based web apps	Perfect for non-developers
N8N, Lindy.ai, Gumloop	AI workflow automation platforms	Perfect for non-techies

LEAP SCORE	**The Assets Ladder LEAP Score calculator is available as part of my career programs on my websites.**

TOOLBOX

There is a tool for every job you have to do. If not, create it.

What's your LEAP Score?

The goal of The Assets Ladder LEAP Score (Lifetime Earning & Assets Potential) is to help users estimate their lifetime work-life potential. As you plan career moves and leaps, these projections should help educate and motivate you to think beyond salary. Meanwhile, most career advice still focuses on job titles and salaries only. But in today's world, your greatest opportunities may come from what you own, not just where you work.

The LEAP Score is a modern metric for measuring your total career value, not just by salary, but by the full earning power of your work and assets over time. It's made up of two parts, which reflect your true earning capacity, both from the time you trade and income from assets you create.

Lifetime Salary Potential: The total income you're on track to earn across your working life, based on your current (or projected) salary, roles, and years of work remaining before retirement.

Asset Income Potential: The projected value of income from assets you create, like digital products, intellectual property, equity in startups, licensing deals, content libraries, online courses, etc. Income can also be derived from the sale of assets.

The LEAP Score helps you:

- See your career as a portfolio, not a single job
- Set smarter goals for both income and asset creation
- Understand how today's projects can compound over time
- Make better decisions about work, collaboration, and ownership

This new metric can be helpful to workers planning decades rather than just thinking about the next job. It helps side hustlers estimate the real potential of opportunities over the long term. For career coaches, the LEAP Score can help ensure your clients measure meaningful, long-term success from all possible incomes, not just one job at a time.

Sample Simplified Calculation

Estimate an annual pay rise.

LEAP Score = Salary Earnings + Asset Income Potential
Salary x years to retirement €75,000 x 25 years = €1,875,000
Asset Income Potential e.g. Online courses, royalties, IP
25 years x €20,000 = €500,000
Plus revenue from selling ownership of assets
LEAP Score = €2.375M+

17. MY STORY

You are never too young, or too old, to start

My entrepreneurial spirit emerged early in life in Ireland. As a teenager growing up near Oldcastle, Co. Meath, I made my first investment by convincing my dad to let me buy a calf for our family farm. A year later, I sold the calf for a decent profit. That success spurred me on to start my first proper business venture - painting neighbours' houses as a summer job.

Despite receiving a Commodore 64 (C64) computer as a family Christmas gift, I didn't use it much as it pre-dated the Internet. I was more interested in sports than computer games. However, one of my brothers used it to learn programming, which led to a successful international career in consumer electronics. What an impactful present for Fergal!

Later, in the 1990s, after university and several international summer jobs, I recognised the emerging importance of the Internet and online marketing. Despite having no experience or prior interest in technology, I was willing to relocate to Cavan, a small regional town, to secure my first role in sales and marketing at a small Irish technology company.

Breaking into the tech sector marked the start of an exciting career combining technology, business, and culture. Nowadays, I can be found using AI tools to make images of what I might have looked like as a child with a computer.

Experiment 1: Personal Branding

As long ago as 1999, I launched my first personal brand website, pioneering in an area that would later become crucial for professional success.

My career path has never been conventional as I've always believed in combining traditional employment with entrepreneurial ventures. This personal brand even earned me a long-term working visa in Australia, where I spent three successful years before returning to Ireland.

My Personal Brand started delivering for me in 1999.

My early days
Ireland

My first investment was a calf

My first published article was when I was 13

My first business was painting houses

My first award was in school

Bank of Ireland

My first partnership and first business website were in 1998

InsureWeb.ie
For all your insurance needs

My first person brand website 1999 earned m a job & visa in Australia

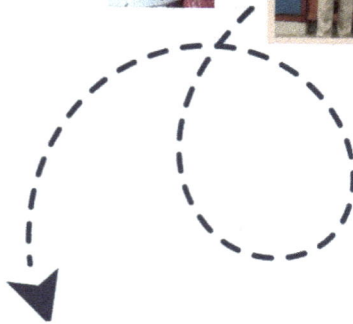

I started from scratch with nothing. No family business, no assets, no connections. No problem.

One of my proudest achievements came with the creation of 'Connector', a personal brand side hustle that evolved into a thriving digital studio business in Dublin. Recognising the absence of a digital community in Ireland, I established one through monthly Connector Meetups, regularly attracting over 120 attendees.

After ten years of building Connector into a digital experiences business for global clients, we grew revenues to seven figures annually. In early 2020, I sold the business to a competitor. However, Connector is still part of my identity. Throughout this book I will share some stories of people I met on my own career journey, people who I think have an interesting career journey too.

Experiment 2: Digital Agency

My goal when I started was to learn and earn and to stay curious. More specifically, to continuously gain new skills in new emerging technologies and to monetise this learning. This overall goal has underpinned my career journey.

As an innovator, I moved my career online in 1997 as one of the earliest adopters of internet business in Ireland. The same happened with Web 2.0, aka social media, as I tend to identify big trends before most of my peers.

My love for connecting people led to a series of 'edutainment' style experiences. By closely watching emerging cultural trends, I was able to design and deliver customised events like the Huawei Irish Instagram awards. The original name I chose was The Instagrammys, but after discussions with Instagram, we were told to avoid using anything with 'Insta', so we settled on The Snapys.

This was conceived and delivered for 500+ guests in Dublin. It was all made possible with a bespoke software platform and our credibility within the Irish Instagram community. Another big corporate event was an EY European Innovation Day event in Switzerland for over 500 professionals. This innovation experience was packaged as the 'Global Innovation Game' and sold outright to a global events company.

Some of my global clients for Connector in Ireland and the UK included Huawei, Sony, Volkswagen, Benecol, Dr. Oetker and L'Oreal.

Personal Brand

My 'Connector' Personal Brand

Awards

Some awards I won in Ireland, the EU and the US.

Experiment 3: Education

What I enjoy most is taking emerging technologies, figuring them out, and simplifying them for others in an engaging fashion. Today, I combine my experience as a course designer (up to Masters level) with years of lecturing, training, and facilitating in marketing and innovation.

As I spotted the emergence of social media very early on, I created a platform for myself as a trainer in this subject. I also created the brand SocialMedia.ie as a platform for me and other trainers for a wide range of clients.

As an adjunct professor in Digital Marketing at Maynooth University for two years, I helped many students create their personal brands for career success. In total, I trained over 5,000 people in innovative marketing practices.

My largest educational project is the book you are reading today. As well as researching, writing, and designing this book, I have also created courses and workshops with gamification elements with a future release date. I love creating innovative educational experiences for clients and my own personal projects.

Careers offer so much potential for engagement, collaboration, and gamification. This book is just the start of a series of products I will launch soon.

Experiment 4: Career Design

Throughout my journey, I've consistently demonstrated that a successful career doesn't have to follow a traditional path. By combining employment, side hustles, and business startups, I've built and sold multiple ideas, brands, and businesses. Now, I'm committed to sharing these experiences and insights to help others design their own unique career paths.

While in Australia around the turn of the millennium, I had a job as an IT Recruiter for many global technology companies. This was a huge learning curve and helped me learn how to identify and nurture talent. Later on, as a CEO, I managed hiring and firing. Mentoring many young international graduates to career success has given me great satisfaction.

During the COVID lockdowns, I took time to reflect on my career journey and began exploring the future of work. I conducted dozens of interviews with Irish makers, movers, and shakers, including many successful self-employed individuals. I released these interviews as a podcast under the project name 'Self Makers'. Subsequently, I launched the 'Future Work World' platform for the European recruitment firm Cpl.

Since 2024 I have organised a series of events in Ireland called 'Career Lab' where large numbers of attendees come to learn how to future-proof their careers. My passion for innovation and sharing knowledge led me on a journey to where I am today. However, I want to use my learnings to help you on your journey of exploration too.

Conor's Map

Conor
Dublin

CAREER PATH

1. New jobs in digital marketing
2. Ends employment
3. New software partnership
4. Starts selling Conman tees
5. Connector digital agency
6. Freelancer and career designer

Career Overview 2000-2030

LEARN: I worked a series of jobs in digital marketing until I had enough experience and confidence to work for myself.

EARN: I had marketing jobs in addition to side hustles selling t-shirts and running events.

OWN: I created a personal brand in 1999, a T-shirt brand, an event series called Connector which became a digital agency.

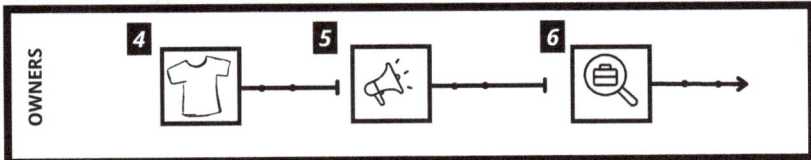

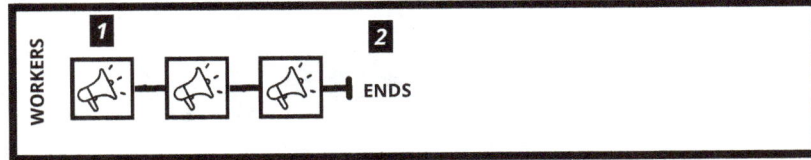

Career Design

As a seasoned experience designer and educator, I created a series of interactive educational experiences to bring this book to life. I want to reimagine career education for individuals and career collaboration for groups.

Get in touch for your customised workshops or to buy a Career Design Toolkit.

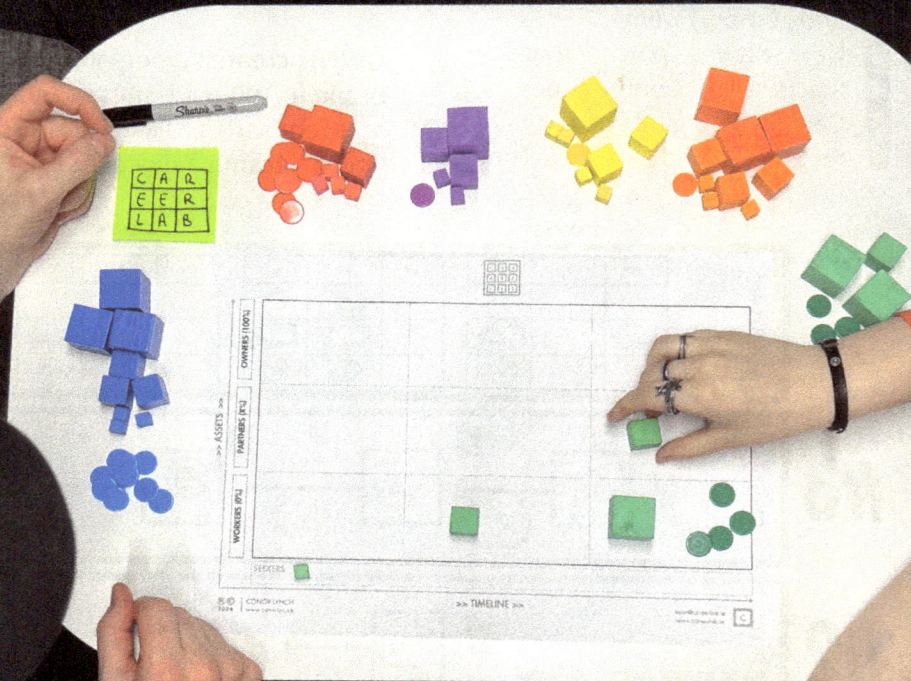

18. CONCLUSION

Take ownership of your work

Your career is not a job. It's not a title. It's not a CV.

It's a collection of choices, compounded over time, that define how you spend your energy, grow your skills, and shape your life.

We've grown up being taught to follow rules, wait our turn, climb the ladder. But today, the world of work is faster, flatter, and more fluid than ever before. Technology has removed the gatekeepers. Markets have become global. Anyone with a phone, an idea, and internet access can build something meaningful.

And yet most people are still stuck playing by old rules.

This book isn't about quitting your job and becoming a digital nomad. It's not another glorified side hustle. It's about something much deeper: ownership.

Ownership of your reputation.
Ownership of your energy.
Ownership of your work.
Ownership of your assets.
Ownership of your potential.

You've seen examples of people who conceive remarkable businesses while working full-time. These are not superheroes - they are simply people who learned to work differently. They built while learning. They created while earning. They used the system to fund their own escape from it. They are rewriting the rules of work. You can too. But not by waiting for permission.

The linear career path is dead. It's no longer about climbing a single corporate ladder. Instead, think in terms of platforms, projects, and personal economies. Think in terms of assets - not just salary.

What sets apart high-impact workers today isn't just intelligence or credentials. It's creativity, initiative, adaptability, and the ability to build - products, content, connections, systems, tools, or teams.

Every personal project sharpens your skills.
Every online presence becomes a digital asset.
Every collaboration, article, side business or niche idea you test becomes part of your unique career fingerprint.

This is not a game of job titles - it's a game of accumulated momentum.

Start small, think big

You don't need to know everything now. You don't need a master plan. You just need to start.

- Start with your first career experiment
- Launch your first learning project
- Create your first income-generating asset
- Start designing a career that reflects who you really are - not just who you're paid to be.

The tools are in your hands. The stories in this book show it can be done. And your biggest advantage? You're reading this now - while most others are still waiting for someone to tell them what to do next.

Success today belongs to those who think like entrepreneurs - even if they never launch a company.

They know how to:

- Learn, earn, and own
- Create something small but valuable
- Show their work
- Build networks of collaboration and trust
- Stack assets, not just hours
- Learn in public

Your job might pay the bills. But your career assets - your skills, ideas, relationships, and projects - are what will build long-term wealth, freedom, and impact.

Your 20s are for learning. Your 30s are for earning. Your 40s are for owning.

Steven Bartlett

Move to The Assets Ladder model

There's a compelling argument for shifting focus from the traditional, rickety old Career Ladder to The Assets Ladder model. By prioritising the creation and ownership of diverse assets, individuals can build long-term income streams and increase their earning potential, moving beyond the limitations of trading time for money.

This paradigm shift requires a conscious effort towards asset creation, effective time management, and leveraging personal skills and networks to build a more resilient and prosperous future. All delays are costly when you can improve your earning potential today.

In a world where anyone can do almost anything, where there are infinite ways to learn, earn, and build - what will you do?

The tools are cheap. The risks are lower than ever. The upside? Limitless.

Start to experiment now. Build momentum. Design your future by owning the present. And remember: your career is not a path to follow - it's an engine to build.

Remember that the career cycle compounds. A Learning Project gives you new skills. That skill fuels an Earning Project, which creates income. Over time, the income and experience evolve into an Owning Project— something that lasts beyond your hours.

Then the cycle repeats: the freedom gained from ownership allows you to invest in more learning, which sparks new earnings, and so on. Each turn of the cycle strengthens your independence. Over time, you build a diversified career portfolio: part employment, part collaboration, part ownership.

In the information age, the cost of inaction is going up, because the cost of action is going down.

Nicolas Cole

The final word

As you can see, the future of work is changing for those blessed with human or artificial intelligence. This book is for the readers of the human variety, but machines are also welcome to digest and reflect on these ideas too as they grow more sentient.

The goal with The Assets Ladder and the 'Learn Earn Own' career projects is to help you succeed with multiple career paths, rather than being ignored and stuck on a single rung of a Career Ladder.

My Career Design methodology is inspired by Design Thinking, whose human-centred design principles should help you design better careers and assets.

DAVID + STEPHEN FLYNN

THE HAPPY PEAR

The Flynn brothers launched The Happy Pear as a small fruit and veg shop in Greystones, Ireland, while working abroad. It grew into a café, natural foods store, and online platform, employing up to 200 people. Revenue peaked at €10.6 million in 2019.

PARTNERS

WORKERS

THEHAPPYPEAR.IE

Big decisions need to be made about the risk taken in being but a cog in a heartless machine. Decisions need to be made fast, as every day's delay has a compounding effect on your lifetime earnings and asset potential. Why wait until next year to kick off a learning project if transformation is needed? Why wait to start collaborating? Why wait to improve your work life?

I hope you enjoy this book and know that there is much more to come from me. My personal website (www.conorlyn.ch) is a good place to stay in touch with new developments, including books, eBooks, workbooks, courses, templates, workshops, webinars, and games.

With the development of prompt-based software programming, my Lifetime Earnings & Assets Potential calculator and other useful tools are much easier to create. I'm excited to spot trends, create apps, test these ideas, and collect some data to analyse.

My career journey has been circuitous and colourful, and I am happy to share all I know to help you with your career adventures. I wasted time on costly trial and error as I stumbled on my unplanned career path, but now you can pre-plan your career portfolio using my tools.

I hope you will visit my digital home and find interesting content that shares new ideas and shows these ideas in action. And don't forget, a book review means the world to me.

Let's go!

Linear careers go nowhere fast. It's time to redesign careers.

The Multi-Career Starter Kit

Discover three different possible futures you could build from your current skills, including one multi-career path. The Multi-Career Starter Kit is a short, powerful exercise you can probably complete in an hour or two.

This exercise requires no complex planning or long-term forecasting. All you need is your current CV, a simple AI prompt, and The Assets Ladder map template. You bring your CV, and I provide the rest.

Work is changing too quickly for any single career path to feel certain. For many people, this creates anxiety: What should I do next? Am I falling behind? What if I make the wrong choice? But uncertainty becomes easier to navigate when you can see more than one possible future. Instead of feeling stuck, you gain perspective. Instead of constant doubts, you begin to design.

This experimental process works well for ambitious people who are unsure where to focus their energy, and equally well for individuals who fear making the "wrong" move. By exploring multiple futures, your mind relaxes. You stop viewing your career as a single high-stakes bet and start seeing it as a series of small bets.

Expand your career activities with a Multi-Career - work for others, with others, and for yourself to create multiple income streams and assets. Multi-Careers, or Portfolio Careers, involve holding multiple, complementary roles. These are growing as an accepted career model rather than a niche path.

The goal is not perfection. It's clarity through contrast. When you compare three possible paths side by side, something becomes obvious: one of them feels more exciting, more aligned, or simply more "you." I recommend you choose the one that best helps you to learn, earn, and own. However, you decide!

Step 1 — Upload your CV

Copy and paste your CV into ChatGPT or any AI tool you use. It doesn't need to be polished or up to date. AI works well even with messy or brief information. Add in any career goals you have, or any other likes/dislikes, to help personalise the results for you even more.

Step 2 — Use the Career Mapping Prompt

Paste in the following prompt and let the AI generate three future career paths based on your skills, experiences, and strengths:

I want you to analyse my CV and generate three distinct 3-year career paths I could follow. Here is my CV: [Upload CV] [Insert career goals, likes/dislikes etc.]

Please output:
1. A "Predictable Path" – what my current career naturally leads to.
2. A "Pivot Path" – a more ambitious or creative direction using my transferable skills.
3. A "Multi-Career Path" – a portfolio of 2–3 complementary roles or income streams I could build at the same time. For each career path, give:

- A 1-line title, e.g. 6 words
- A short explanation (100 words max)
- The 3-year progression (Year 1 / Year 2 / Year 3)
- Key skills to learn
- Income opportunities I could unlock
- One small action I can start this week

Within seconds, you'll receive three futures: one familiar, one stretching your abilities, and one blending multiple roles or income streams. Most people are surprised by how many possibilities their existing experience can support.

Step 3 — Choose the career path you prefer

Which option sparks curiosity? Which one feels expansive rather than restrictive? Which one feels worth becoming the kind of person who could do it? Choose based on energy, not fear.

Step 4 — Sketch it onto the Assets Ladder Map

Turn to your map for the next three years — 2026, 2027, and 2028. Under each year, think about:

- Skills you will learn
- Income you will earn or expand
- Assets you will create or begin
- Your roles (Worker / Partner / Owner / Multiplier)

I am omitting the Seeker's role so everyone can focus on being active, rather than inactive.

Keep this exercise high-level and intuitive. You're not writing a detailed plan — you're designing a direction. For example:

2026 - Roles: Worker + Partner + Owner (Multiplier)
2027 - Roles: Worker + Partner + Owner (Multiplier)
2028 - Roles: Partner + Owner (Multiplier)

Learn: AI tools, Automation, and Course design
Earn: Paid workshops and Consulting Services
Own: Digital Products, Templates, and apps

Step 5 — Review your Assets Ladder Map
Below, I show a Multi-Career with three concurrent Career Roles, simultaneously active as a Worker, Partner, and Owner. However, you can print the template multiple times, one for each career plan you are prototyping. For even better results, print out your map and place it prominently where you can see it often. Then update your goals and milestones regularly so you can see your progress.

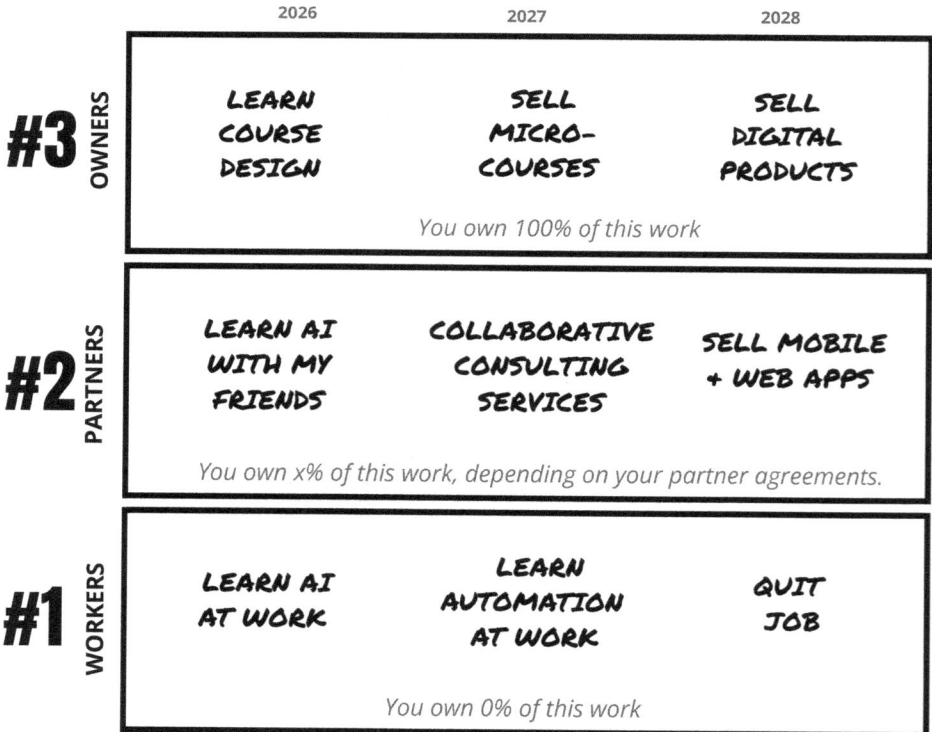

		2026	2027	2028
#3	OWNERS	LEARN COURSE DESIGN	SELL MICRO-COURSES	SELL DIGITAL PRODUCTS
		You own 100% of this work		
#2	PARTNERS	LEARN AI WITH MY FRIENDS	COLLABORATIVE CONSULTING SERVICES	SELL MOBILE + WEB APPS
		You own x% of this work, depending on your partner agreements.		
#1	WORKERS	LEARN AI AT WORK	LEARN AUTOMATION AT WORK	QUIT JOB
		You own 0% of this work		

The Multi-Career Starter Kit

Here is your blank template. Other templates are in the book and available on the book website.

	2026	2027	2028

#3 OWNERS

#2 PARTNERS

#1 WORKERS

BOOK EXTRAS

Thank you for reading my book. It means a lot to me. I hope you will find it a valuable resource to open your mind to new ideas and opportunities.

There's something special about having a practical, personalised playbook in your hands, where you can highlight your favourite quotes, mark key sections, take notes, and write down your new ideas. My maps are designed for you to keep as a visual reminder of your journey to career success.

You can get a free Templates PDF to download from the book website. It contains the book templates and some additional pages for you to use while you read the book and design your new career options.

Review the book

I'd love to hear your thoughts about the book. Leaving a good review on book sites like Amazon not only supports my work but also helps others discover the book. I want to help people like you have more successful working lives, and you can also help by leaving a review or sharing the book.

Scan the QR Code to review this book on Amazon:

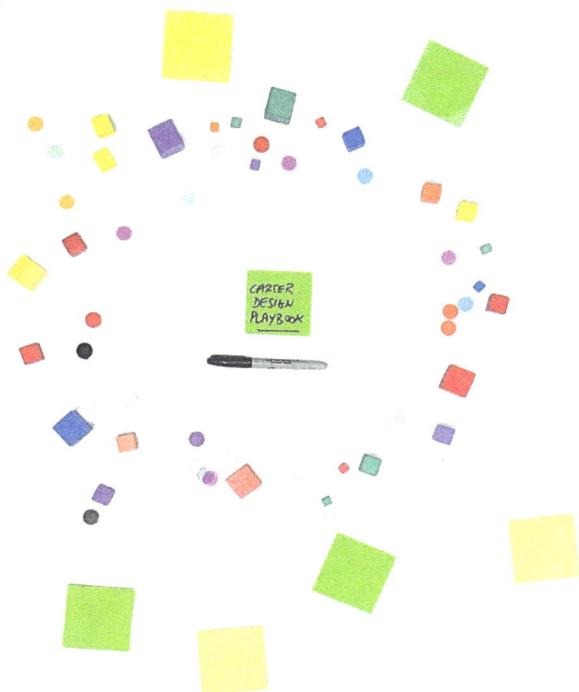

The Assets Ladder book is the first part of a series of practical Career Design knowledge products, including books, webinars, courses, and original workshop activities like games.

Blank templates and other resources are available on TheAssetsLadder.com. Collaborate with others using The Assets Ladder toolkit for your own group sessions.

Register on my personal website www.conorlyn.ch to receive an email newsletter featuring trends, talent, tools, and transformative thinking.

Create with me

If you would like to discuss these ideas further, I'm available for interviews, presentations, and collaborations etc. If you would like me to personally help you multiply your potential one-to-one or in a group, get in touch to discuss plans and projects. Email me on conor@conorlyn.ch to take your career to the next level.

Want to help others design their perfect career?

If you are like me and want to help others design their perfect career, this book is your first step into new ways to engage with those you want to help. There is nothing better than helping others to be happier and healthier as a result of having an enjoyable and fulfilling work life.

So if you work as a 'Career Professional' e.g., a career coach, guidance counsellor, teacher, advisor, or social worker, this book and toolkits are for you too. Maybe you are interested in human resources and talent management and want to give the best advice to people?

This book is part of my contribution to addressing the tragic waste of human potential and happiness associated with poor career choices. The Assets Ladder may be for your personal use, but it can also be very useful for engaging with others on a casual or professional level. I have created and tested workshops and games you can run with small or large groups.

You may not have qualifications in careers or business, but this book and my other tools and templates are hopefully as accessible as they are actionable. Contact me if you are open to becoming a 'Career Designer', which can be an interesting addition to your profile.

As well as this book, there are lots of other resources I will release for those whom I call 'Career Pros'. Follow me on my websites where you can also get in touch with me about becoming a Certified Career Designer.

Linear careers go nowhere fast. It's time to redesign careers.

REFERENCES

This book draws inspiration from a variety of entrepreneurs, thinkers, writers, and creators. Below is a list of works and authors cited directly or quoted in the text. Thanks to all the people showcased.

Books

- Priestley, Daniel. 24 Assets. Create a Digital, Scalable, Valuable, and Fun Business That Will Thrive in a Fast-Changing World. Rethink Press, 2017.

Articles / Reports

- Eurofound / Adapt Report 2022, via EU-LFS (Labour Force Survey).
- Gallup. State of the Global Workplace Report. Gallup, 2023
- Goldman Sachs Creator Market Research 2023
- IDEO. "Design Thinking Defined." IDEO.org, 2020
- MBO Partners / Emergent Research "State of Independence in America 2023" (published in early 2024).

Quotes & Sayings

- Alex Hormozi 2022 - x.com/AlexHormozi
- Ali Abdaal, Facebook April 9, 2025 - aliabdaal.com
- Arie de Geus, "Planning as Learning". hbr.org - March 1988
- Bill Burnett & Dave Evans, Designing Your Life - 2016
- Codie Sanchez - tiktok.com/@realcodiesanchez
- Cal Newport - CalNewport.com
- Dan Koe's newsletter, October 2024 - thedankoe.com
- David Autor, Massachusetts Institute of Technology (MIT) - 2025
- Derval O'Rourke - Interview with Conor Lynch in 2020 - derval.ie
- Ed Giansante 2024 - www.linkedin.com/in/edugiansante
- Greg Isenberg 2025 - x.com/gregisenberg
- Helen Tupper and Sarah Ellis, Squiggly Careers, amazingif.com
- Joshua Cohen, Apple University, University of California, Berkeley
- Justin Welsh 2024 - x.com/thejustinwelsh
- Mark Tilbury 2024 - MarkTilbury.com
- Naval Ravikant - various content - nav.al
- Nicolas Cole, various content - nicolascole.com
- Richard P. Rumelt, "Good Strategy, Bad Strategy", 2011
- Reid Hoffman, Forbes, August 26, 2024 - reidhoffman.org

REFERENCES

- Russell Brunson, various content - russellbrunson.com
- Sam Altman, Fortune, February 4, 2024 - samaltman.com
- Sarah Chrisp, Entrepreneur.com, February 19, 2020 - wholesaleted.com
- Shaan Puri 2022 - x.com/ShaanVP
- Simon Sinek - simonsinek.com
- Simon Squibb - Instagram, July 28, 2025 - simonsquibb.com
- Stephen Bartlett - stephenbartlett.com
- Terence McKenna - terencemckenna.com
- Tim Carden, various quotes - x.com/timthoughtleadr
- Warren Buffett - various interviews
- Unattributed quotes are from the author

Inspiration (Not quoted)

- Business Model Canvas - Alex Osterwalder & Yves Pigneur
- My First Million - Sam Parr & Shaan Puri
- Seth Godin - various books and content

LEARN
EARN
OWN

THE
ASSETS
LADDER

THEASSETSLADDER.COM
WWW.CONORLYN.CH
CONOR@CONORLYN.CH

www.ingramcontent.com/pod-product-compliance
Lightning Source LLC
Chambersburg PA
CBHW071420210326
41597CB00020B/3581